Outdoor Yarns & Outright Lies

Gene Hill and Steve Smith

STACKPOLE BOOKS

For our kids, Jennifer and Patricia Hill, and Amy, Christopher, and Jason Smith. Not only do they tolerate our comings and goings, they even take a little time to smile with us.

Copyright © 1983 by Gene Hill and Steve Smith

First published in paperback in 2007 by
STACKPOLE BOOKS
5067 Ritter Road
Mechanicsburg, PA 17055
www.stackpolebooks.com

Printed in the United States

First paperback edition

10 9 8 7 6 5 4 3 2 1

Illustrations by Tom Hennessey

Cover design by Caroline Stover

Library of Congress Cataloging-in-Publication Data

Hill, Gene.
    Outdoor yarns and outright lies.

    1.Hunting—Anecdotes, facetiae, satire, etc.
I. Smith, Steve. II. Title
SK33.H6594   1983   818'.5402   83-8159

ISBN-13: 978-0-8117-0698-8; 978-0-8117-3427-1 (pbk.)
ISBN-10: 0-8117-0698-2; 0-8117-3427-7 (pbk.)

Contents

Preface

I had the honor to call Gene Hill a friend for two decades, collaborated on a couple of books with him, was his editor on a couple of different magazines, got drunk with him, and laughed and cried with him. Most of the really good stuff we did together I can't share, at least not in a book that may inadvertently fall into the hands of small children.

That aside, I had the pleasure of shooting with Hilly in a number of places for pheasants and ducks and quail. Hilly always had some observation, some way of looking at something having to do with gunning that was pure, distilled experience and wisdom. He was a first-class shot, but he considered me his equal in the field. I am here to confess that I am not and was not. I earned his respect the old-fashioned way: I swindled him. Maybe "swindled" is too harsh a word; it was more like "deceived." Allow me to explain.

It started off innocently enough. We were shooting pheasants in Iowa, at a very high-class shooting preserve. The birds were plentiful, flew grandly, and offered great sport in the stout prairie wind. I found, twenty minutes out of the lodge, that it was one of those days when I couldn't hit the ground with my gun if I dropped it—we've all had it happen to us. Hill was shooting well, as was his custom, fast and accurate and deadly. So as the morning progressed, I worked my way over until I was next to him, behind the busy shorthairs, working the cut milo fields.

I dropped a fired hull in the right barrel of my gun. When a bird went up, Hill would shoot it, I would snap the trigger, and when he'd glance at me as the dog retrieved the bird, I would open the gun and the ejector would snap out the "fired" shell. Like two world-class shotgunners with lightning reflexes, we had doubled on the bird, two shots from two guns going off as one, neither man hearing the other's shot because of his own.

I did that the rest of the day, claiming a half-kill on each of his birds. The faster he shot to beat me, the faster I "shot." Now, to sell my scam, I'd make self-deprecating little remarks—ones that were technically true but misleading, you know, like Clinton's. "That was your bird, Hilly. I'm sure I didn't hit it." Of course, he thought I was being generous and sporting. He looked at me with newfound respect.

A couple of years later, in Mexico, Hilly and the late Dave Meisner, our partner on a number of such outings, were shooting quail. There were a lot of birds. We were shooting the autoloaders the outfitter provided (no taking a fine gun into Mexico—not unless you wished to donate it to the Federales' Retirement Fund), and instead of loading three shells, I'd load two. When Hill dropped a bird, I'd just reload as he watched me. I'd smile or shrug my shoulders and silently claim his bird (I'd slip the shell out of the magazine later). When he shot a double, I'd make a show of loading one shell and palming another. He'd just shake his head. If he ever suspected me, he was too much of a gentleman to accuse me, and I was having too much fun with it to stop.

I remember screwing him over in another way on a duck shoot, also in Mexico. Hill was a great waterfowl shot, and the outfitter set us up on a small pond the pintails were using. It was late January, and the birds from the north were down and using the ponds and fields. There were scads of them. On that trip, Gene's wife, Cathy Lee, joined us, along with Meisner.

The evening before, under the influence of strong drink, Hilly commented that even though he was too modest to make a big thing of it, he wouldn't be too offended if we wanted to refer to him as the Pintail King, describing in great detail how he would execute difficult crossing shots, high passers, and those tricky dropping incomers. This violated one of Hill's Shotgunning Precepts: Brag about your shooting after the hunt, not before. And, of course, he was going to have to pay for his mistake.

The next morning found us in two blinds—Meisner and I in one, Hilly and Cathy Lee in the other—maybe fifty yards apart. As luck would have it, nearly all the birds passed by our blind, and Meisner and I lowered a number of them. Hill's only shots were at screamers that were approaching from behind him, out of the morning sun. By the time he got on them, they were well out and moving away, difficult at best. That day, Hilly found them impossible.

Finally, he screamed over that we should, from our better vantage point, for once in our miserable lives, do the honorable thing and let him know when a duck was approaching so he could stand and take it before it got past him. We hooted at the Pintail King but agreed. Five minutes later, a duck came screaming at his blind. We waited a bit too long before alerting him, and he missed. . . . Three times. He gave Dave and me—by now convulsed with laughter—a rousing verbal whipping for "deliberately withholding information" about when the just-missed bird was within shooting range.

Now, he was in rare form, and he swore to us, to Heaven, and on the grave of his sainted mother that the next bird was a dead bird, or his name wasn't Gene Atkins Hill, the Pintail King. We promised to give him more warning.

Hunkered back down in the blind, he did not see the next bird coming, of course, relying upon his friends to do the right and principled thing to save his day and what little remained of his reputation and tattered self-esteem.

As a bird approached, Meisner and I gestured frantically while hunkering down, each pointing at the bird with one hand and making stand-up motions with the other. Hill stood up in a twinkling; he pivoted, mounted his gun as smooth as butter, squinted into the sun and absolutely centered . . . a curlew.

Meisner and I almost fell out of the blind laughing. Hill looked at the dead, hapless shorebird floating on the pond, looked at the gun, and looked back at us, as crestfallen as I had ever seen anyone. Around the plug of chewing tobacco in his cheek, he muttered an unprintable oath in our direction. Meisner and I had, by this time, run out of oxygen from laughter. We called him the Curlew King. We asked for his autograph. We asked for the empty shell, so that we could have it bronzed. Did he want the bird mounted? He finally looked at us, his basset hound face creased with a grin, and started to laugh. And laugh . . . that hearty, Scottish–New Jersey laugh. A laugh I'll never forget.

I'll also never forget the phone call he made to me that dark afternoon from his hospital room, a call to say good-bye, when the cancer was eating him up, and he was wracked with pain. He wanted to tell me himself that it was time—wanted me to hear it from him. I was glad to be on the list of those he reached out to, and the courage of that one simple act will stay with me if I live to be thirty-thousand years old. Two days later, Cathy Lee called with the final word, and the earth became, in an instant, a less friendly, inviting place.

He's been gone ten years. We have not seen one like him before, and I doubt we will again. To those who read him and learned from him and loved him—even if they never met him—his passing marked the end of an era. I never knew anyone who loved outdoor writing who wasn't a fan of Gene Hill. He had no peers, only admirers.

He had a thousand friends. I'm glad I had the chance to be one.

The Preseason

For quite a few years, whether we've been that aware of it or not, we've had what you might call a preseason. In fact there are a couple of them. For gardeners it's January when the first of the seed catalogs start to arrive with their unvarying promises from which most of us get very varying results. But it's delightful to be able to imagine yourself with a wheelbarrow-sized pumpkin and a cellar full of all sorts of preserves while the winter winds claw at the clapboards and the hoeing and weeding backaches of last summer are lost to memory. Even though by no stretch of the imagination could I be called an enthusiastic gardener, I still enjoy poring over descriptions of dream gardens and landscapes that would be the envy of a Hollywood mogul.

No less magic is the late summer arrival of fall as envisioned by our more famous suppliers of the very latest in hunting boots and ducking parkas guaranteed to keep the lowest of Fahrenheits and the wettest of squalls from chilling our fervor or dampening our enthusiasm. I love that first arrival and cherish the thought of sneaking off to the hammock slung deep in the shade of two towering sycamores where the distant sounds of my wife hoeing weeds in the garden fill me with a tranquil peace. I quickly leaf through the pages searching for the one or two items that I know are there that will be virtually indispensable for the coming season. (Last year it was a Gore-Tex parka in camouflage lined with Thinsulate.) Certain *must orders* crop here and there—can always use another chamois shirt, a new pair of heavy wool socks, new long johns, a couple of red bandanna handkerchiefs, a 28-gauge, leather shell belt and a flashlight—basic yearly orders as necessary to the psyche as flour and salt were to the well-being of the Hudson Bay trapper.

Underneath the hammock I can hear the puppy snoring, exhausted from worrying the weeds thrown out on the lawn from the garden. Add new collar to list. Put catalog down as a slight change comes over the air. Maybe it's something some genius has put in the ink but I could swear there's a little smell of autumn in the air.

The idea of sleeping for a few weeks and waking up just before bird season suddenly has a great appeal—just before bird season but just after leaf raking and storm window season. As if reading my mind the weeder is calling from the garden and I put the catalog in my hip pocket and wander over. The X-ray eyes that women develop a few months after marriage do not fail even in the fading light. "What is it that you can't live without now?"

"Nothing, really," I say. "Might get some socks and a new pair of long johns since you seem dedicated to shrinking my old ones. The one sock that I can find is about the size of a baby's mitten and I'm still old-fashioned enough to prefer them in matched pairs. Anyway I brought the catalog over in case you see something you need if I decide to order a couple of things."

"What I need is to find what the puppy did with the trowel and for you to water the pepper plants." I see instantly that this is not the best time to discuss an early Christmas present and I talk the puppy into coming with me to get water. I ask the pup what she's done with the trowel and don't get a civil answer from her either. Women are all alike.

Make a mental list of possibilities depending on present condition of certain items and whereabouts of others that are believed lost. Other items highly desirable but out of financial reach; useless to put them on Christmas list as wife, children stoutly refuse to believe that I don't have three of everything anyone has made in the past ten years. This is partly my own fault as I have steadfastly refused to throw anything away that has even a faint spark of life left in it; the question of new hip boots is guaranteed to start an argument as the uninformed, or rather stubborn, cling to the erroneous belief that I have about six pair, where, in truth, the one pair that I have for duck hunting are almost twenty years old and I only continue to wear them because I haven't found anything I like better and I honestly want to find out just how long they'll go on, since, as you know, the life expectancy of this kind of footwear is a couple of seasons at the most. The others leak beyond repair, are not insulated, and one of these days out they go! But, to be on the safe side I better make it a public ceremony complete with a farewell address. . .

Then there are always a few marginal items that, given a little time, can be more or less justified. Leather belt, because old ones are a) shabby and b)leather shrinks. Cartridge holder for 7mm Mag because old one seems to have crawled off the shelf where I left it. Alarm clock—old one seems to have stayed in some duck camp, which reminds me to look around for old Swiss army knife. Probably no great harm in ordering one just in case.

After supper the puppy wants me to go out and play and it suddenly occurs to me that I'll try something new. I get out my one good pair of hip boots, the twenty-year-old ones, and taking a handful of training bumpers wade out into the pond.

It worked perfectly. When the little dog brought the dummies back to me she put her front feet up on the boot tops and scrambled for some kind of hold; in half an hour the old boots looked like the start of a salad. The pup had had more than enough of this and we walked back around the yard a couple of times so we could both dry off before coming back into the kitchen.

On the tour the puppy had somehow found the missing trowel and we paraded somewhat triumpantly inside. My wife looked at both of us and smiled as she retrieved the trowel. "Turn around," she said to me. And as I did she asked where the boots stood in my rotation system. I said that this was my number one pair. She handed me the catalog that I'd left in the kitchen and said, "When you order the new boots, get me a chamois shirt. I've marked the page."

When I took the pup upstairs to put her in the kennel in the bedroom, I made sure I wasn't being followed and put my old leather belt on the floor. If there's one thing a pup can't resist it's chewing on an old leather belt.

Gene Hill

The Vet

Among the experiences a man shares with his hunting dog, the thoughts of days afield, exquisite points, or flawless retrieves through gale winds and smashing surf are probably the first—and most pleasant—to come to mind.

Yet, there are other experiences, ones we allow to fleet only briefly across our collective psyche. These experiences are less than memorable, and, in truth, are often harrowing for both man and canine. Topping my personal list of these dubious days of dogdom is a visit to the Vet.

Now, a dog that can't, after three years of yard training, learn the meanings of the words "come," "whoa," and "heel" will learn, after one trip to the pooch health parlor, not only what the word "vet" means, but he will learn to spell it as in: "Catch the dog because I'm taking him to the v-e-t." After this statement, Sport vanishes like snowflakes in a campfire.

A dog you thought couldn't smell a grouse if the bird moved in with him can smell the alcohol/disinfectant odor of the vet's office from 300 yards upwind.

And, a dog that has impeccable field manners is reduced to the four-footed equivalent of a juvenile delinquent within microseconds of entering the waiting room. In short, the average dog desires a trip to the vet as much as his owner covets hemmorrhoid surgery.

So that I will not be accused of making all this up, I have decided to set down in print the latest bout I had with my faithful, nonslip, English pointer, Toby, during a recent trip to the Vet. I have recorded all times and events as they happened with no embellishments. See if this doesn't sound like your typical trip. Since I was busy most of the time, my notes are cryptic at best.

8:45 a.m.—Announce to wife that it is time for booster shot to be inflicted on Dog. Wife laughs in high-pitched, somewhat hysterical manner, her left eye starting to twitch.

8:47 a.m.—I locate Dog under bed in the spare bedroom, paws wrapped around bed frame and glazed look on eyes. I must take bed apart to separate Dog from furniture.

9:12 a.m.—Dog and I arrive at Vet's office. Dog holds onto steering wheel of Jeep as I attempt to remove him from vehicle. I am amazed at strength of this animal, strength of steering column of AMC vehicles, but disappointed in strength of new leather leash which breaks in scuffle.

9:15 a.m.—Enter Vet's office. I am dragging Dog behind me with remnants of leash. Dog pushes ahead of him three metric tons of gravel from Vet's parking lot due to the fact that he has not taken a step since leaving Jeep. I tell little teenage receptionist that I am here and wait while she pulls Dog's file and places it on desk. I notice that Dog's file is the only one of all those assembled with large black spot in upper right hand corner. I comment on this, and receptionist smiles wanly and excuses self to answer a phone which I could swear wasn't ringing.

9:20 a.m.—Seated in waiting room, I try to read magazine (circa 1948). Dog attempts to pick fight with male half of a matched pair of grey French poodles. I separate animals after Dog has shredded hand-knitted sweater that Pierre (for this is the name of the beast) is wearing. I note with some relief that Dog has not perpetrated any ungentlemanly acts on Fifi, the female half of the poodle tandem.

9:21 a.m.—Dog attempts ungentlemanly act with Fifi. I intervene, prevent this mishap, and get glass of water for female owner of poodles who apparently suffers from an asthmatic conditon.

9:26 a.m.—Dog has suddenly become a model of decorum, resting between my feet on the floor. Decorum has something to do with the recent entrance (at 9:25) of a Great Dane with the physical dimensions of large, chest-type freezer. Dane lies at his owner's feet and glares at Dog, who has taken a sudden interest in his toenails.

9:35 a.m.—I enter Vet's examination room. I wait quietly as Dog eats draperies suspended from window frame. Vet enters and asks me to place Dog on slippery, stainless steel examination table. Dog likes this about like I enjoy pulling my own teeth. Finally, I catch dog (thanks to small size of room) and place him on table. Vet approaches.

9:38 a.m.—Vet notes that Dog is disgustingly healthy and will no doubt live many years. I am unsure of how I should take this news, as Vet tels me this with no discernable enjoyment. Vet approaches with Parvovirus serum in syringe. Dog looks as though the Second Coming has arrived and all the good hiding spots are occupied. I grapple with Dog. Vet grapples with Dog. Vet drops syringe. Vet glares at me and Dog. Dog glares back. I turn away and examine what is left of drapes.

9:41 a.m.—Vet has fresh syringe and look of determination—nay, vindication—on his face. Vet injects Dog with technique and enthusiasm akin to that of Olympic javelin thrower. Dog vocally carries on as though an important appendage is being amputated. I comment on this, and Vet notes that this wouldn't be a bad idea, although sound of Dog has covered his words so I cannot swear that he uttered that exact phrase.

9:44 a.m.—Dog and I emerge from examination room and visit teenaged receptionist who—until this very morning—had once entertained dreams of becoming a Vet. I pay bill and leave. As door closes behind me, I hear faint but growing crescendo of applause.

9:54 a.m.—I arrive home and Wife notes that Vet called and I have left remains of leash in waiting room. Vet also told Wife that I needn't return for the leash. He will mail it to me—at his expense.

Steve Smith

The
Primrose Path

There are certain natural laws that we have all learned to live with that are as constant and valid as the fact of gravity. Laws like: "If anything can possibly go wrong it will." "Nothing is impossible to the man who doesn't have to do it." "Never do today what can be put off until tomorrow." "Things are never as bad as they seem—they're usually worse."

Now, what our language is sorely missing is some law to explain the phenomena that happen to the guy who likes to spend a little time out-of-doors. You likely know the pattern all too well. It starts in a variety of ways, but buying a puppy is as common as any. Now, more than not, one of the first dogs you think of is an English setter—just because they're pretty. Then you discover as the dog is growing up that it is pointing the robins on the lawn. So you figure if the dog will point robins, why not take the next logical step and see if it will point quail or pheasants? Unhappily for you—it does.

The next step is borrowing a neighbor's gun and buying a license to take a shot or two to see if the dog can help you pick up a nice bird or so for Sunday dinner. Then it's hunting clothes. Memberships in a local gun club to practice your wing shooting. Then it's discovered that you need at least *three* guns: one for birds, one for skeet, one for trap. Then it's either a lot of expensive trips to find better bird hunting or an expensive membership in a shooting preserve. Now your dog is in heat and you start looking for a good male so you can have just one more dog. Or vice versa.

You now have at least three guns, an enormous wardrobe of gear, memberships in various gun clubs, shooting clubs, field trial, and dog clubs. And you've traded in a perfectly good family sedan for a new station wagon. You start smoking a pipe. You discover that the pleasant smell around the fire in the lodge is only part woodsmoke—the other part is bourbon. You seem to get sick a lot in the fall so you can't show up at the office. You have started to shout "DOWN!" "HUP!" "OVER!" at your children and barely caught yourself in time to keep from telling your wife "HEEL!" Your good suit is always covered with dog hair and so is the house and the car. There are teeth marks in all the chair rungs and your good leather boots. Your expensive shrubbery is a horror and none of the words a preacher uses on Sunday could describe your lawn.

But not to mind. A man can have worse habits than three guns and some bird dogs—not more expensive or time consuming—but there are worse.

Pretty soon a friend of yours will stop over and start chucking your puppy behind those silken ears and begin asking your advice. Chances are you will start to speak with forked tongue, as our Indian friends used to say. You will describe the dawn smell of the meadows with a soft, persuasive voice, speak lightly of your acquired skill with a shotgun and dwell longingly on campfires and twilights as you top his glass with a fresh dash or two. You offer him your can of Brushsmoke to fill his pipe. By now he's too far swept away into some imagined October afternoon to notice that his suit is covered with dog hair and pipe ashes have scorched little holes in his tie.

You lend him your copy of Ray Holland's *Seven Grand Gun Dogs* and Burton Spiller's *Firelight* and send him off to sail by new stars.

It's just another one of nature's immutable laws that we are all bound by. Some might say that it's "Misery loves company." But we know better. It's really more like "God doesn't count the hours man spends afield with friends," or "The thing we build that lasts longest is memory." All we ever need to do to hear the sounds of geese is listen. All we ever need to do to see the point and the flush is to close our eyes.

Gene Hill

Getting in Shape

A long about this time of year, the average grouse and woodcock shooter has finally physically recovered from the season enough to make, once again, intelligible noises.

Among these noises are the kind usually associated with self-improvement. You know, the kind of things you say to yourself while you're risking a bilateral hernia pulling on your boots. Things like "I gotta get in shape!"

Well, last year I made up my mind that the upcoming season wasn't going to catch me off guard, no siree. So, along about last spring, I went on a total self-improvement kick to get myself into shape for the rigors of grouse and woodcock hunting in the upper Midwest.

I might add that, for what passes for a "living," I'm a school teacher. Usually, I do nothing more rigorous than throw out the odd detention slip or stoop to pick up chalk, so my slate, as it were, was clean. Anything I did would be an improvement.

Since then, as now, jogging was in vogue, I decided that this was the way to start. I mean, jogging would be great for getting the old legs in shape for slogging through swales and fighting those thigh-clutching grapevines come the shooting season.

Har-dee-har-har.

Not wanting to appear ignorant of the sport, I watched

the joggers who trudged past my house at semiregular intervals. I watched for about two weeks and finally thought I was ready to enter their company.

I got ready the first morning a little before dawn. Soon my heart was pounding and I'd broken out into a sweat. It got worse once I got out the front door.

Clad in my flannel jammies (I later found out that joggers wear what they call "sweat suits" that only look like flannel jammies from the front window), I took off jogging down the block when the first batch of runners swooped by.

"Took off" is somewhat misleading, unless you compare it to the way the Mississippian glacier "took off" a few thousand years ago.

Rather than give you all the gory details of my time among those pedestrian pain peddlers, I've decided to give some pointers to any other out-of-shape bird hunters who might be considering this form of group lunacy.

First off, jogging is a very enlightening experience. I learned lots of stuff, which I'll pass on to you for nothin'.

Among the things I learned is that joggers don't jog in their L.L. Bean hunting boots. It not only isn't chic, it also hurts like homemade sin. Instead, joggers wear special shoes (which is, of course, a form of cheating) called "jogging shoes." These shoes can be had at almost any retail sporting goods outlet for a price slightly less than the gross national product of Peru.

I learned that every dog with the speed of light, fangs the size of twenty-penny nails, and the disposition of a gut-shot Kodiak all have the following things in common: They will all belong to people who live on your jogging route, they will all be untethered by kennel or leash anytime you are jogging, and they will all look on your thighs the same way Jack the Ripper looked upon some throats in London a few years back. The results are about the same.

I also learned that an out-of-shape bird hunter can do, after a few blocks of this form of masochism, a fair imitation of an eskimo down on all fours calling seals.

I learned that jogging can turn you so red in the face

that cars will stop and wait for you to turn green (which comes a bit later) and that the local witch's coven will worship you from your front porch on nights of the full moon.

Steve Smith

Ski Problem

A fellow I work with has a dreadful illness that reaches its peak during the winter—the man's a skier. I know, I know, it's sad. But the worst part of it is the guy will not admit to himself or anyone else that he's sick! Even at Alcoholics Anonymous they can't help you if you don't admit your problem. Still, I've decided to help this fellow out. He's a good friend and I feel I owe it to him and society to make him aware of his irrational behavior.

At lunch the other day this man (I'll call him Tim) had an attack. I looked outside, and it was snowing. Tim started to salivate—much like Pavlov's dogs—at the mere sight of snowflakes. I guided him to a chair, urging him to blink lest his retinas dry out and become inflamed. He kept muttering "fresh powder" under his breath. It was a half hour before I could calm him enough to talk.

When we talked, it became obvious that Tim spends far too much of his hard earned money on ski equipment. He told me that some types of skis cost over $50 and even more! I, of course, was shocked. That's as much as a good reblue job on my skeet gun! Imagine.

He also said that boots were almost as much, and that the people who own those ski hills actually charge people to go down them. I knew then that Tim was almost beyond my help—he was paying people for the use of gravity. When I asked him why, he stared at me blankly like my beagle does when he rips up the paper and I catch him at it.

"Because it's fun," he told me. "It's a real challenge and thrill to pit yourself against a hill and conquer it."

"OK," says I, "what do you get if you win the challenge?"

"The thrill of winning," Tim responded.

If Tim loses, I found out, he gets compound fractures and beaucoup dislocations of various parts of his anatomy. Gently now, because Tim was once an all-state football player, I asked:

"Let me get this straight. You spend hundreds of dollars and drive hundreds of miles to rent another person's gravity in the hope that you will come out of the whole thing alive?"

"Well, Smitty, that's about as simple as it can be put and I know you're simple," he muttered.

I've given up. Now when Tim talks of his ski excursions I smile nicely, nod, and watch his temples throb. We all have our little idiosyncrasies that make us each individuals.

For you others, though, I've invented a sport that I think will catch on. It uses all the thrills and challenges of skiing. In this sport, you buy a tree—a big expensive tree—use special expensive climbing gear to shinny up the thing, and then hurl yourself at the ground from about a hundred feet and then try to get up to see if the parts all work.

Oh yes, you must pay the tree's original owner for the use of his gravity.

Steve Smith

Friends?

There comes a time in every man's situation when he has to try to lie a little to his children to protect them from certain ugly sides of life until they are old enough to understand. For example, at this time of the year when I'm getting my stuff together to go out and have a few friendly rounds of skeet or trap or shoot a few patterns testing out a new reload I've concocted that mixes 8s with 9s, one of my little girls will ask "Why isn't Mr. Zern or Mr. Rikhoff going with you?"

I simply say that my friends Mr. Zern and Mr. Rikhoff have horrible hangovers and couldn't stand the noise, but the truth is that these otherwise good family men are fishing. I once tried to explain to Patty, my seven-year-old, what "fishing" was. I explained that Mr. Zern would put worms on a hook, that the hook was tied to a pole of wood with a piece of string and Mr. Zern or Mr. Rikhoff would then dangle this in front of a small trout or bass in an effort to catch him. I instantly realized my mistake when Patty, who has been reading the waterfowl regulations, along with wholesome stories from Churchill's *Game Shooting* and Greener's *The Gun and Its Development* saw the thing clearly and burst into tears. I asked her what was the matter and she said sobbing, "But Daddy, that's against the law." I asked her what law and she said section so-and-so, paragraph so-and-so.

I hurriedly looked it up and found that she was referring to the federal laws against baiting. I tried to explain to her that it *did* seem like that but it really wasn't. And to further clear her mind I went out and got some hair bass bugs Jim Rikhoff had forgotten the night he was helping me test the specific gravity of some apple cider (the same night he drove all the way home with the emergency brake on and had to have the drums freed with a welding torch). I told Patty that certain men thought that if instead of using real bait they used what they called artificials (as hair bugs certainly are), and this was the epitome of being sporting. She got the idea right away, although not at all pleased that the men she had admired for their ability to make light of her father's whiskey and endure the rigors of predawn goose pits and blistering August afternoons at Vandalia, Ohio, had this character flaw. So, a little depressed at my lack of success at shielding her from these ugly facts of life, I watched her disappear into her playroom. A few hours later she came running into my study where I was busily putting a little linseed on a few scratches in my Krieghoff stock.

"Daddy, we're rich, we're rich!" she shouted. And opening a cigar box she showed me what she'd been working on. In the box were some beech nuts, and some corn kernels, perfectly made of colored modeling clay and even a long roll of serrated earth-colored clay that made a fairly good imitation of an earthworm. I asked her what she thought she had. She said that if we made artificial corn, artificial beech nuts, and fake worms, why couldn't we attract ducks, grouse, and woodcock? That really wouldn't be baiting, it would be using artificials, and we could go into business and make bushels of money, which she thought (having listened to my wife's frequent discussions on the subject) we sorely needed. I explained to her that it wasn't the sort of thing a real bird shooter would stoop to doing, legality notwithstanding. I also pointed out that she had once seen Mr. Rikhoff drink a rum cola and so he was not to be trusted with an idea like plastic corn and that we would just forget it. But somehow the picture of Jim Rikhoff and Ed Zern holding up a brace of pintails and saying how they "took them over half a peck of hand-made plastic Golden Bantam" sticks gloomily in my mind. Will the federal authorities please advise?

Gene Hill

Ice
Fishing

One of the reasons I have remained so ignorant of so many of the things going on around me is that I spend so much of my time staring up in the sky or peering down trying to make out what's going on in the water.

It was a natural thing that I should take to ice fishing; it's one of the most perfect outdoor pastimes for a born loafer. Where else can you spend most of your time rotating your carcass around a good fire, scorching and steaming in turn, and looking down through a hole watching for fish and still look busy?

Besides the active loafing, ice fishing had a lot going for it. First there was the discussing stage that covered where, weather, and the general preparation. The next step was to put the chains on the Model A. That was one of my jobs because, for reasons I don't remember, one rear tire was a little larger than the other—so if the first set of chains went on relatively easy you knew you had the wrong chain on the wrong wheel. A really successful job of getting chains on always left you wet, frozen, and with bleeding fingers—there was a lot of satisfaction in that job I can assure you; when it was finished you felt and looked like you'd been doing something! The second phase was going out to look for bait. We were particular about getting the right kind of shiners and getting the right size. Most people used saltwater killies, but we felt that they weren't big enough, lively enough, or hardy enough. It had to be fresh-caught local shiners. And you had to go looking for them. We had a telephone of sorts, but it didn't matter much whether it worked or not since almost no one else had one anyway. We'd go out driving around and buy six or eight here and maybe a dozen someplace else—each and every one discussed and handpicked. I know it sounds crazy, but I had "pet" shiners that I wouldn't let anyone else use. They just looked better to me.

Pop always scorned store tip-ups as extravagant and impractical and inefficient. Instead, we cut sticks of lakeside willow or alder about two feet long, made a little slit under the bark, and after sounding the water, slipped the line under the slit, so the shiner would be as deep as we wanted it, and tied a little piece of red rag in the line below the slit. When a fish took the bait the red flag simply disappeared, and we knew we had a bite. Further, if it simply got too cold or we stayed out on the lake too long we just left the sticks in the ice.

Every so often I got fancy ideas and would make a few tip-ups out of lattice board and old corset stays, but I really liked the little willow sticks a lot more. I don't remember ever seeing anyone else use the kind of setup we liked, and I've always wondered why. They were foolproof, free, and a lot easier to move and carry. And they kind of made you feel a little bit like you were living off the land—or could if you really had to.

The only hard part was cutting holes. My bad reputation about being careless with edged tools carried well over to the old ax we used for fishing through the ice, so I almost never had to cut the holes. Further was the argument about how big the hole should be. I leaned toward optimism, and if I was allowed to cut my own holes they turned out to be about three feet across. Not only was that sheer fantasy, but somewhat dangerous, and it took me so long to cut a hole that big I'd never have gotten more than five or six lines in. And the old ice ax was the only thing we ever used—no matter how thick the ice. You often got wet using it on the last few inches of really thick ice, but it did a nice, neat job, and somehow it seemed important to have it look just right.

Our lines were heavy cord; I seem to remember that we used plumbline and dyed it green. Each line was about fifteen feet or a bit more in length with a hook on one end and a loop on the other. The hook of one line fastened through the loop of another and the whole business of twenty or so lines was (being in one piece so to speak) wrapped around a big notched board with a rope handle for carrying. I figure that the whole business, so far, had to cost less than a dollar. The only other extras were the red rags, a dipsy sinker for sounding and an old wire strainer we used for skimming the ice out of the holes as they froze. The whole business was carried in a wicker basket, with the blue quart Thermos full of tea with honey riding on top.

As soon as the holes were cut and lines set out I was itching to build a fire. And you have to know that the kind of kid who would cut a three-foot hole to catch a pickerel you could pull up through a jug would have to build a fire so big and hot no one could get near it. If all the wet mittens I burned up trying to dry them were laid out end to end—I'd deny it!

I usually ate my lunch before nine o'clock simply because I liked getting exactly the right toasting stick cut and couldn't wait to use it. I never cared too much for toasted onion sandwich, really, but there was a strong belief going around in those days that raw onions keep you from all sorts of dread diseases. I never contracted any dread diseases—so who knows? If being wet and cold was unhealthy I never would have seen the ripe old age of twelve.

So here we are. It's ten in the morning. On the shoreline roars a hardwood fire, and we are spread out in some loose formation that is intended to cover varying depths of water (my favorite set or two in the deepest part where I was wrongly convinced the big ones dwelt) and nothing happening. Time to skim the holes and jig the shiners just a bit to wake things up. And somehow, in all this random world, one hole would assume a special something to my eye. I'd sneak my favorite shiner on that one hook—and watch the red rag like a hawk. Then, before too long, I'd find myself with my hat brim in the water, hands shading my eyes just so, watching what went on underneath in that dark and lambent world. A world as fascinating—or maybe more— than anything I've ever seen. A world of cold shadows. A world of infinite mystery where I could imagine pickerel the size of oars and bass as big as hip boots.

But happily, it is more often that not the fish that are never seen that keep us coming back to fish again. Real fish are not the ultimate fish, no matter how big—we are convinced that deep down there swims something bigger.

The great thing about fishing is that we almost never know. And all we really learn from peering down through our hole in the ice is the everlasting magic of simple wonder.

The last set of willow sticks we ever used is sitting in a bundle tied with binder twine in a very special corner of my room. A faded picture of my father cleaning pickerel on the ice hangs right beside them. The rest is lost—except the hollow thunk-thunk sound of the ax biting into ice, the still-young happiness that comes with staring into a dark green world that I will never understand, and seeing the old plumb-line go taut. And then, as if by magic, comes the charging monster pickerel that still lives there, beneath the ice—a dream that is as new and old as fishing is itself.

Gene Hill

The
Answer Man

Among my more noble traits, I take time to answer my mail with regularity. Naturally, my reputation as "The Answer Man" has preceded me; spread, no doubt, by the crowned heads of state with whom I am acquainted and regularly consult.

I thought I would share some of these questions and answers with you in the hope that your hunting/dog-training skills may be heightened.

Dear Steve,
    I am just taking up shotgun shooting. What is the single most important piece of advice that you give me?
Fred

Dear Fred,
    Don't put your mouth over the end of the gun barrel.

Dear Steve,
    I have heard of the notion of training a hunting dog by the use of a bell, much as Pavlov did in the early part of this century. I am especially interested in getting the dog to eat by the sound of a bell, as did Pavlov, so I can set a timer and go away for the weekend, leave food available, and know the dog will be well fed.
Henry

Dear Henry,
    I don't know. When I was a kid, my brother and I trained a Great Dane to eat like that at the sound of a bell. The mutt ate the Avon lady.

Dear Steve,
    I am just taking up outdoor photography and am in the dark (so to speak) about some of the terms used. Please define: "lens," "lens opening," and "ASA."
Herbert

Dear Herbert,
    Gladly. "Lens" is the glass gadget in the front of the camera. "Lens opening" is what happens when you drop the glass gadget on your driveway. "ASA" is a man's name, not popular since the 18th century (much like "Herbert").

Dear Steve,
    What is your opinion of toy poodles?
Jack

Dear Jack,
    They're delicious, especially with wild rice.

Dear Steve,
    Every time I take my pointer bitch hunting, she blinks on birds and refuses to hunt. What makes it worse is that my wife is on me about giving the dog away and spending my Saturdays in the fall cleaning the garage, washing windows, and splitting firewood. What should I do?
Randy

Dear Randy,
    I'd suggest that the next time this disgusting trait surfaces, you slap an electric shock collar on her and run electricity through her until she cooperates, then spray her with a hose and make her sleep in the kennel all night sopping wet. I don't know *what* to tell you to do about the dog.

Dear Steve,

I've recently taken up fishing and have a question to ask. I thought I'd ask you because I don't want my pals to think I'm a fool for not knowing the answer, and I know that that never stops you. What is a "surface plug" in regard to bass fishing?
Jim

Dear Jim,

A surface plug is what one gets if you are bass fishing and chewing tobacco at the same time. Eventually you'll get sick of the plug of tobacco and spit it out, and tobacco floats. Simple? By the way, if a bass hits while you're chewing, you'll find out the meaning of "diving plug."

Dear Steve,

I was in a fishing store the other day, and the salesman asked me what kind of net I use. What does this mean?
Nestor

Dear Nestor,

Well, first off, you're badly mistaken about the term 'net'. It is not a fishing item, but is the store's margin of profit. For example, the $150 fly rod you bought cost the store owner 12 bucks.

Dear Steve,

When I go fishing, I am troubled by canoes that come splashing around the bend every few minutes or so. Is there any way to stop this short of finding another place to fish?
Pete

Dear Pete,

Yes. Buy a department store mannequin and take it with you. When you see a canoe coming, start giving the dummy mouth-to-mouth respiration on the stream bank. Canoeists will see this and paddle for help—usually upstream from where they came because they are not overly bright. Once they've gone, continue fishing. They won't be back until you're done fishing—if you hurry. Another way is to invest in small portable water mines similar to those used in WWII to protect sub pens. This, of course, is a last resort because explosions can hurt the fish.

Dear Steve,

Every once in a while, my wife accuses me of spending too much time and money hunting and fishing. Can you give me a good argument about why I should be allowed to go hunting and fishing every Saturday all year?
Joe

Dear Joe,

No.

Dear Steve,

What is the best method that you've found for getting a bird dog to stop eating the birds that he's supposed to retrieve to me?
Charlie

Dear Charlie,

Before the hunt, force-feed him a Jersey cow. If the trouble still persists, try feeding him one of my wife's apple pies.

Dear Steve,

What one tip can you give me that will help me to be more successful on my deer hunting trips?
John

Dear John,

If you don't have a pair after four cards, fold.

Dear Steve,

I'm curious about the term "belton setter." Please enlighten me.
Dick

Dear Dick,

This refers to a training method often considered harsh,

much like "larruping Labs, "punching pointers," "chastising Chessies," "beatin' Brittanies," "boppin' Boykins," "sockin' springers"—had enough?

Dear Steve,

I'm a little advanced in years, and when my young Britt goes into a blowdown to point a grouse, I always climb up on a log so I can see better. Then, after the bird flushes, I find I can't get down off the log. Any suggestions?
Rodney

Dear Rodney,

Sure. You don't get down off a log; you get down off a goose. (Say "uncle.")

Dear Steve,

I recently acquired a dog called an English setter and took it into the field to see if it could find game birds for me. Instead of flushing any birds, it would stand real still and stiff until I came up to see what was wrong, at which point a bird would break from cover, scaring me half to death. What should I do to cure this fault?
Hank

Dear Hank,

Whenever I've had a dog with this disgusting affliction, I would wait until he stopped and stiffened and then I'd sneak up and kick him as hard as I could (wearing tennis shoes so as not to injure the beast). Usually a week of this type of intensive training will cure the fault.

Dear Steve,

Hunting aside, what is the best stunt you've ever trained a dog to do?
Wifred

Dear Wilfred,

Chew through the cord on my kid's stereo.

Dear Answer Man,

I hired a guide named Mortie to take me pheasant hunting while I was in a well-known pheasant state. Mortie demanded his money up front and then left, promising to meet me later. He never showed. What gives?

Iggy

Dear Iggy,

I don't know, but I think I met Mortie's sister once in Kansas City.

Dear Steve,

I want a light gun capable of killing pheasants. How much will such a gun cost me?

Mark

Dear Mark,

A gun capable of killing pheasants costs $39. A light gun costs $100. A light gun capable of killing pheasants costs $4,890.

Steve Smith

Memories of
Misses Past

It's sort of traditional at the end of the year to look back
and take stock of what has happened during the last 12
months. One friend of mine keeps a diary. The regular
kind, you might have seen one, for hunters and shooters.
But a diary is pretty matter-of-fact. You sit around with a
couple of your shooting buddies and one of them says,
". . .that was the day you had the double on green-wing
teal. . ." Without a diary you can agree and return the com-
pliment with something along the line of ". . .yes, that's
right, I remember it well because it was just two weeks later
you had a 94 at Grouse Ridge Gun Club. . ." and the evening
is warm with the passing of such soft and sweet memories.

But with a diary this never happens. The diary reveals
that not only did you not double up on green-wing teal on
that particular day (you did not one time double on anything,
all year), you missed four easy incomers flaring out over the
decoys and went home with two sea ducks. The diary would
also reveal that George M. did not get a 94. The diary would
read that as usual George M. was stopping his gun and
lucked into an 87. The diary is to the shooter as the scale
and tape measure are to the fisherman—irrefutable proof that
the judgment and memory of the outdoorsman improves,
like a fine wine, with the passing of time.

We're not in the business of facts and figures, anyway.
Nobody's keeping score. Our end of the year inventory can

have anything on the shelf we want. Two ruffed grouse can become eight or even ten or twelve. If you count the near misses, perhaps even a trifle more. The weather along the Chesapeake can get a lot colder and windier when you're sitting in front of a log fire a month later.

So instead of taking a long, hard look at the times gone by, let's take a softer, dreamy one. Why not put your feet up on the good furniture and see what you'd like to have happened. This is nowhere near any form of lying—that's an art in itself. We're just looking at the truth from a variety of angles. Did Old Ben break into a covey of birds and flush them out of sight or do you suspect that he hit a running bunch of birds and did damn well to put them up so you could mark down the singles?

Did you really miss that huge old gander that came sailing in on set wings or did you just fire way behind him on purpose—sort of a parting salute? Did you really end up with only a 17 on your last round of trap or were you "working" with the gun to test the width of the pattern? Give it a little thought and you'll discover some nice smooth lines to shore up your story.

I know one shooter who can barely hit the ground with his hat and after his usual two-shot miss he waves his gun barrel around very happily and says "Boy, that's what I'm out here for, just to see 'em fly!" He's carried on like this for so long that even *I'm* tempted to believe him. Trapshooters who have a long string of zeros will talk about how they're just polishing timing and rhythm. And one of the stupidest bird dogs I have ever seen is constantly praised by his owner for his "range."

So, look back and see what fits—from a different perspective. And next year start giving your Christmas presents early. Comment in admiration on some shooter's rhythm and timing. Slap your buddy on the back next time his dog busts every bird for a square mile and tell him how much you hate those close-working dogs that are always right there almost under your feet. And when we're together and it's one of those days when I'm a little bit off, it would be a kind thing for us to chat about sportsmanship and the bigger meaning of being out-of-doors.

Gene Hill

The
TBSSM

For all of you grouse and woodcock hunters, and the man who pursues his pheasants in their newfound brushy haunts (compared to open fields), let's talk today about the nemesis of all of us who have to pop brush to find birds: the Two-Barrel-Sucker-Shot-Miss.

For the uninitiated, let me explain that these birds are normally hunted where cover is very thick. Seeing a bird is, in itself, a feat. When it comes time to do something serious about it, mainly shoot, the plot thickens.

The gunner must locate the bird, determine the course the bird is using for escape, mount the gun, swing smoothly, establish the proper amount of forward allowance, pull the trigger, and keep swinging.

Down in the brush, all of this is happening while branches are slapping you in the head, thorns are seeking out your eye sockets, and one foot is balanced precariously on a fallen log. Add a little wind and a half-broken dog that likes to chase birds, and you get the idea why grouse costs about $850 a pound when all expenses are factored in.

Surprisingly, many people connect with great regularity. I know a few who are phenomenal with a smoothbore in the thick stuff. In fact, many of the best average something like two grouse for every five shells, or one woodcock for every two shots—really.

The problem is the above-mentioned Two-Barrel-Sucker-

Shot-Miss. This occurs when the birds mentioned here suddenly and without warning decide that they should flush in the open and fly straight away from the gunner, the easiest shot in the book. Strange and bizarre things can happen at such times to experienced shots. One gent I knew was unable to pull the trigger on such chances. He'd missed so many of them that his psyche wouldn't allow more humiliation and things just refused to happen.

The reason, obviously, is that one's partners take no end of delight in ribbing you about your TBSSM. Old market gunners dreaded this shot because it looked so easy, but long experience in the brush had prepared them for different shooting conditions. The wide-open chance was foreign to them and many missed it.

A while back, I was hunting woodcock. The dog moved in on point, and I stepped into an opening to get a better view as my partner moved to flush. The bird came out high, curved left, dropped to eye level and flew away straight at moderate speed across the opening. What followed? My hands got clammy, I lifted my cheek from the stock to get a better view (sin), jerked the trigger—twice—and there was my annual TBSSM. My partner is still laughing and the dog is still mad at me.

Therefore, I'm rechristening the TBSSM the Expert's Miss. Only good, experienced brush shooters miss such shots. If you can miss this chance, you qualify as an expert. No applause necessary.

Steve Smith

Stiff Waters

Ice fishing season is here as cold weather has hardened the warm waters of Michigan's lakes into something that must be pounded through in order to wet a line. Now right off I'll tell you that I'm not a real devout ice fisherman. I can think of many ways to spend a winter day, and this comes somewhere at the bottom of the list.

I do, however, enjoy getting out once or twice a year, mostly to observe tbe characters who ice fish seriously. I've found they come from all facets of civilization, and in shapes, sizes and ages to baffle the imagination.

A couple years ago, my brother, Eric, talked me into going ice fishing with him and his father-in-law. I went because there was little else to do. I found out a lot about ice fishing that day—all of it bad. I found out that you don't even try to cut a hole in the ice until you are out of sight of land. This means a six-mile forced march carrying enough equipment for an assault on Ice Station Zebra.

I also learned that no matter how much clothing you wear, it isn't enough. I wore everything I owned—down vests, down jackets, long johns, felt-lined boots, two hats, gloves and mittens, and a 3-piece suit my wife bought me for funerals. Still not enough. I almost froze.

I learned that ice fishermen can be devious. While complaining about the cold, Eric told me he had seen some guys stay warm by running across the ice. I tried it and had taken five or six strides when he tackled me from behind like a defensive cornerback. He said that if he could ever find somebody stupid enough to run, HE kept warm by tackling them.

While spudding a hole through the ice, I looked with envy at the fishing shanties scattered around the lake. Some looked nicer than the house I live in.

I saw one with a television antenna sticking out, and in one shanty the smoke poured out of the chimney so furiously that the inhabitants were standing outside in shirt sleeves cooling off. When I grumbled about this, they said I should go ask to rent the basement. This is an ice fisherman's way of telling you to keep spudding—something like "shut up and deal."

I finally got my hole cut, and dropped my line into the dark depths. A fish nailed the bait, and I anticipated a hefty struggle on the short rod Eric had given me. Not so. I hauled in a fat perch which fought little and promptly froze into a finny letter "C" shape on the ice. I found out that the sport in ice fishing is in the contest of staying alive until it was time to quit. The more I looked at that fish, the more I could see myself.

About six in the evening, we decided to head for the car. Actually, I decided to head for the car and threatened the other guys. They sort of looked at each other, packed up, and sat down on the ice. I sat down with them because I didn't know what else to do. Finally, it got about full dark and the lights on the shoreline started to come on. They jumped up, grabbed their stuff, and headed in. They didn't know which way the shore was and they had to wait for the lights. THEY DIDN'T KNOW WHICH WAY THE DAMN SHORE WAS!

Well, that's enough of that. Next year, I'm planning to look at all of my ice in a glass while I spend my winter days trying to find out what it is they print on the bottom of Jack Daniels bottles.

Steve Smith

Telling Lies

After I'd been out shooting chukar partridge with Larry Dinovitz, the head man of the Rocking K Ranch in Bishop, California, we got together over what the cowboys used to call "tongue oil." And as things got along in conversation, Larry got to telling lies about his Labrador, Charlie. And I got to telling lies about my Labradors, Tippy and Judy. Larry, being a gentleman at heart, started out easy with half-mile retrieves and I countered with three-quarter-mile retrieves—on doubles. Then Larry mentioned that Charlie's work on these half-mile retrieves was on giant Canada geese and I added that my three-quarter milers were through a couple of inches of ice. Well, Larry's dog got going nearer and nearer to Alaska and mine got to plowing through stuff that the Coast Guard icebreaker *Eastwind* would flinch at and we started to call it a draw. Larry mixed another batch and suddenly Charlie rose up from under Larry's feet behind the bar and started to bark. Larry said, with a straight face, that Charlie was pretty good at mixing drinks and was reminding him that he had forgotten to add the Triple Sec to the Margueritas. I didn't say anything, Larry being the host, but I really don't believe that *any* Labrador retriever can tell the difference between Triple Sec and Cointreau. Even mine.

Gene Hill

The Stuff We *Really* Need

I don't guess that it's slipped your attention, but the things we really need, the thing that would go a long way toward making our outdoor lives productive and enjoyable, just aren't offered by the outfits that make those fancy catalogs up and mail 'em out.

I mean, think about it. Every season of the year, we get inundated with offerings from L.L. Bean, Orvis, Delta Arms, Dunn's, and a whole raft of other places that got our names from God knows where. Now, these mercantile outlets are wonderful establishments, and cater well to the needs of the *average* outdoorsman, but where are they when we need them? It's enough to make you wonder.

So, with the *real* outdoors in mind, let's take a look at some things we'd all like to see offered in a no-nonsense outdoor catalog.

Now granted, the below-listed items may violate conscience, local ordinances and an odd commandment or two, but I still think we oughta have 'em.

ACME SKYBUSTER RESETTLEMENT KIT

Ever have problems with the guys in the next blind taking 150 yard drags at geese that would have come into your decoys? Ever notice that the same slobs are also great at throwing their lunch bags and other litter about? Would you like to alleviate this unsavory situation?

Then send in your order for the Skybuster Resettlement Kit. Just attach the tube to the hull of your duckboat, line the offender up in the sights, press the red button (provided) and your—and indeed, his—troubles are over. Comes with three torpedoes which should be enough to establish your reputation and still keep you within federal waterfowl regulations which allow only three shots.

Kit also serves off-season duty for putting to route noisy, college-kid canoers on your favorite trout stream. $299.95

MUTT DAZE

Can you remember the last time Old Mindy presented you with a batch of surprise puppies? Bet it was about three days before grouse season opened, right?

Fear no more. Just take our aerosol-powered can of Mutt Daze to the kennel, whistle up old Mindy, and give her a blast. The resulting smell makes every male dog in the neighborhood look at her the same way you'd view Sylvester Stallone in drag.

Price is only $4.99. (Some as-yet-undocumented use on teenaged daughters.)

LARYNX RETARDANT

This 21st century product is a cure-all for the nemesis of all outdoorsmen—bragging. You know how it is, about the time you comment that your dog or shooting (or fly casting, etc.) is second to none, you have one of those off days—with plenty of witnesses.

Larynx Retardant reacts with the hormones released into your blood by the adrenal gland. The release usually precedes bragging or boasting, but also can be used selectively to keep you from opening your big mouth about anything.

Imagine the situations: No longer will you brag about your dog and then have him not only eat all the birds, but also eat the back seat of the car; no more will you be physically allowed to comment that you almost always break 99x100 at trap—to the new Club Champ; never again will you agree to go on a goose-hunting trip to the Arctic Circle in a pup tent with anyone named "Brucie." $23.00

MANDRAKE THE MAGICIAN HYPNOTIC GESTURING COURSE

A booklet which allows you to gesture hypnotically just like Mandrake. Within an hour after reading the booklet, you too can make others see what you want them to see.

Just think—miss a grouse, GH to your comrades, and your miss becomes a snappy right-and-left double. GH to your wife, and the Ithaca Century trap gun you're sneaking into the house becomes a table lamp. Slap a GH on your boss before bird season and he actually *sees* that skin rash of yours (and you take opening week off). Wow. $36.00

FAKE CASTS FOR ALL OCCASIONS

Tired of punching brush? Tired of camp chores? Tired of holding up your end of the outdoor duties? Try the Fake Cast. The foam rubber arm model makes sure your pals cut the firewood at deer camp. The rubber leg cast makes sure you get the premo position on a pheasant drive—standing at the end of the cornfield. It oughtta be illegal! $33.00

OUTDOOR JARGON TRANSLATOR

No sportsman who travels to his hunting and fishing should leave home without this one. It takes the statements of guides and locals and translates them into verbiage you can understand so you can be ready.

For example, if an Iowa farmer tells you that he saw pheasants about, "a half-a-mile thataway," you consult the Translator and find out you better be prepared for a hike that makes the Bataan death march look like a stroll to the privy.

The Translator can also tell you that when a Down East waterfowl guide tells you you're going, "a little ways offashore," you had better pack food, four day's worth of fresh water, and shark repellant.

When an Oklahoma quail hunter tells you that his pointer, "runs big," the Translator will tell you that by the time you get to the dog after he points, the birds will have paired off and nested. $45.00

THE CLEVELAND AMORY LOOK-ALIKE KIT

Ever have a tough time being recognized from the chair at your sporting club's annual meeting? Have you raised your hand and been ignored while the same guys drone on endlessly about the department's policies and the "good old days?"

Then you need our best attention getter: The Cleveland Amory Look-Alike Kit. Comes with rubber mask (complete with moles), "Save Bambi" T-shirt, and a lifetime supply of frizzy, fiberglass hair. Guaranteed to get you the attention you want. Forward proof of hospitalization insurance with order. $32.00

Steve Smith

Dear
Diary:

In the past few years, there has been a proliferation of diary-type books on the out-of-doors. In the main they deal with nature observations and tend toward poetic expressions revealing how the author felt about the changing of the tide, the appearance of the first myrtle or violet, or the arrival of the house wrens. In general these are both pleasant and informative to read, but in truth I find them a little on the "best possible world" side where in reality life just isn't quite like that—at least mine isn't.

A typical diary of mine for December could, of course, include my casual observations on nature, but the reality, the stuff we have to live with would be a little different.

December 2: Woke to find the ground covered with four inches of snow. Remembered that snow tires are still in the barn. Looked for snow shovel and was told that the last time any one had seen it I was using it to clean dog run. Looked in dog run; no shovel. Decide to go buy another if I can get car out of driveway and have garage put on snow tires. End of driveway plowed in by county plow. Spend rest of day in sullen mood. Mocked by owls most of night.

December 8: Last week's snow has generally melted. Have purchased new snow shovel; snow tires on car and new anti-freeze. Feel completely prepared for come what may. Good day to split wood knowing that the colder the day the easier the job. Look for splitting wedges. They are not where I *know* I left them. Look for and find good axe. Attempt to split wood with axe alone; axe stuck three times out of five. Return to barn to look for wedges again. Find mouse tracks leading to ten-pound bag of grass seed which is now four-pound bag.

December 10: Woke to loud cooing of mourning doves—about an hour before wanting to get up. Start day in sullen mood. Forced to buy splitting maul and new wedges. Bitter cold—good day to split hickory tree killed by lightning past summer. Find old wedges in stump where someone had left them. New maul marvelous tool but hard on back. Reminded again why all old farmers are cranky—backs always hurt, people are always moving their things from where they left them.

December 12: Woke to loud honking of Canada geese—about an hour and a half before wanting to get up. Start day in sullen mood again. Decide that one of the wonders of nature is that anybody who lives in the country gets much sleep at all. Bitter cold. Wonder if anybody remembered to shut off and drain water in barn pipes, knowing too well what to expect. Decide to wait until spring to replace burst pipe faucet thus giving me all winter to find where they left my big pipe wrench. Fingers half frozen from fooling with pipes. Debate about having whiskey before noon. Win debate. Less sullen now.

December 15: Woke to immense and deadly silence. Too quiet to sleep. Get up in sullen mood to find six inches of snow and still snowing. Back still sore from splitting hickory and mention snow shoveling to wife; quote statistics of men having fatal coronary from doing same. Wife reminds me of who spent day last week shoveling out duck blind, lugging decoys, and chopping ice. All the bluebirds of happiness in my life have permanently retired south.

December 18: Woke with wrenching backache. Ask wife for breakfast in bed, hopefully waffles with maple syrup. Hear shocking language from wife. Drag self from bed of pain; make own breakfast: two hot dogs, Bloody Mary. Feel better and call faithful retriever to go for walk; looking for Christmas trees. Find one bootlace missing, toothmarks on boot top put finger on faithful retriever, AKA Maggie. Lace boot with string, somehow not the same feeling. Have fine walk: pheasant tracks, deer tracks make snow seem less deadly; almost pleasant. Choose Christmas tree without measuring due to the natural eye of woodsman.

December 21: Awoke to smell of waffles, comforting sound of daughters arguing. Find that argument is who is going to wear my wool shirt. Settle quickly. Find bucksaw in record time and cut Christmas tree. Faithful retriever approves every move. Surprised to find tree three feet too tall for living room. Argue with daughters about shortening tree: top vs. bottom. Compromise. Go to gun club meeting to avoid argument about lighting tree. See four deer in driveway, hear geese overhead.

December 23: Up early to write Christmas list for shopping. Mind blank. Would like to buy wife case of trap loads but lack courage. Daughters get wool shirts; tempted to buy size 46 but lack courage. Also give musical daughter duck call on theory of "who knows?" Decide to buy wife hip boots. Brave decision, lingering doubts; throw in wool shirt and thermos bottle. Give other daughter goose call. Big Dipper seems close enough to touch. Hear more geese overhead; a sound to thrive on.

December 24: Go shopping. No hip boots size 6. Buy size 12 and write note explaining. Wool shirts OK. Calls OK. Thermos OK. Buy case of trap loads for "family" present. Feel generous. Excited; can't wait to see wife's face. Outside, owls calling winsomely—for owls; they are about nesting time—

agree that there is not much else to do now—good thinking. Wouldn't mind being owl.

December 25: Woke to duck and goose-type sounds coming from living room. Heart full of joy—make mental note to buy girls camouflage coats for next birthdays. Faithful retriever jumping on bed—loves sound of duck. Come downstairs, find wife wearing wool shirt, hip boots—pours coffee from new thermos. Hands me packages. Down vest, size S, note saying store out of XL's. Get nylon bone from faithful retriever, case of trap loads from girls. Splendid! Little Christmas tree at breakfast plate decorated with new salmon flies— new fly line—tell family they are too generous to me, family agrees, but smiles. Take faithful retriever for walk, try wife's new boots—perfect fit. Mourning doves in old apple tree— one of softest sounds to reach man's ear.

December 28: Awoke to sound of faithful retriever chewing shoe. Daughters arguing. Sullen mood suddenly lifts: special lunch day at the gun club! Look for long johns, heavy sweater. Need high-carbohydrate breakfast: 100 trap/100 skeet. Have new theory to try at both—secret method. Exciting prospects; whole new era may begin now. Troublesome wind at club badly affects new theory. Saw three crows in driveway on way out: bad luck. New theory still exciting—tell wife, girls; swear to secrecy. Girls giggle; do not take life seriously enough. Running low on wood. Debate brandy after supper. Win debate. Fall asleep in front of fire.

December 31: Woke to smell of hot biscuits and coffee. Feeding chuckle coming from back bedroom, not bad. Good breakfast: ham, redeye gravy, grits, biscuits, etc. Get chainsaw fixed first thing. Cut wood for stove, fireplace. From distance see house in different perspective. Warm lights, girl playing piano, Christmas tree colors, faithful retriever eager to see fireplace. Wait a minute or two and pretend to be stranger. Think happy people live there. Hear owl asking WHO? WHO? and answer ME! ME! Remember to sweep snow off boots before entering kitchen. Forget to brush faithful retriever. Wife says didn't expect me to be perfect. Smell roast duck cooking. Debate about martini before dinner. Win debate. Win everything.

Gene Hill

Gunsmiths

Would you like to know what there is to like about gunsmiths? So would I.

This creature, necessary to those of us who gun and are never—but never—satisfied with the stocks, locks, and chokes of off-the-rack shotguns, is a bane on the life of every shooting man.

I don't mind going to a gun shop to pick up a box of shells, buy my license, or even gossip about the upcoming woodcock season. That stuff I can handle.

What bothers hell out of me is when I get a notion in my head that this or that gun would shoot a little better for me with this or that done to it. Not major surgery, mind you, just the usual things you have to have done to a gun to make it just right: a little more/less stock drop, a little more/less choke, a little more/less weight in the right place, et cetera.

Anyhow, when you walk into a gun shop—the known habitat of gunsmiths, you are immediately at their mercy.

First off, they always want to know why you gotta have done what you want done. Always. If you try to explain, they just sort of roll their eyes back in their heads, tell you that you really need something completely different (and more expensive) performed, and then sort of chuckle about sports like us who are never satisfied. Apparently, it never occurs to them that if it weren't for unsatisfiable sports like us, they'd still be changing the oil on Chevies down at the Amoco station like they were before they took that correspondence course.

Like all professional guides everywhere, they have no truck with any gun that does not—down to the scratches in the wood—exactly duplicate what they shoot.

And, to hear 'em tell it, they shoot those guns well. Twelve grouse with twelve shots is about standard for a three day hunt, hordes of waterfowl for the expenditure of a box of shotshells, and woodcock? Hell, they're so easy that a gunsmith doesn't even shoot at 'em anymore—hasn't since he was a kid.

If you ever bring a high-grade double to most of these guys, be sure you pay your last respects before you walk out the door. To give you an idea of what the feeling is like, pretend that you're saying so long to your oldest daughter who has taken a mysterious position on Bourbon Street at a place called *The Rising Sun*. Get the picture?

Gunsmiths are always accompanied by cronies who evidently have nothing else to do (like earning a living—your tax dollars at work) and are possessed of IQ's only slightly higher than the melting point of ice. These guys stand around, listen to what you want to have done, and then guffaw and allow as how the old Marlin single would do everything just as good as that there 20 gauge-with-the-name-he-can't-pronounce-what-comes-from-Italy.

He and the gunsmith have some type of symbiotic relationship. The gunsmith uses him for a foil and as an audience when he really wants to show off for a sport, and the dummy uses the gunsmith as a way of being near and accepted by the great and the near great.

Let me give you an example of how this tandem works. Witness the following visit by yours truly to a typical gun shop, occupied by a typical gunsmith. The characters include myself, gunsmith(GS), and the local moron(M).

Self:(entering shop) "Hi, Jim-Bob. Got a gun I want you to take a look at. Maybe you can help me out. She's shooting a little high for me, and I think about an eighth-inch off the comb would do it right up."

M:(interrupting) "Lemmee see that thing. How do yuh say this-here name? Bernuhdaily? Hell, this gun looks okay tuh me."

Self:(ignoring Moron) "What do you think, Jim-Bob? Can you have that done for me sometime before the next ice age?"

GS:(looking at gun) "Hell, Sport, that ain't cher problem attall. Yer real problem is that the barrels on this little ole thang are a way too long. Yud oughta let me cut 'em off fer ya and give ya wide-open chokes."

M:(slapping his blue jean-encrusted thigh) "By gorry, Jim-Bob that's jest what I was gonna say, yessiree."

Self: "Look, these chokes are custom-bored cylinder and modified. This is my best woodcock gun, my early-season piece. The 26-inch length is just right. If I cut off the barrels, the balance will be ruined."

GS:(rolling his eyes) "Look, I'll carve up yer stock if that's whatcha want," (I cringe at the use of the word "carve") "but I'm tellin' ya that cut-off barrels is the only way tuh go."

M:(pointing at Gunsmith) "Yeah. What *he* said."

Self: "Look, I want the stock done. How much?"

GS:(strolling over to the window so he can see the make, model, and vintage of my car) "Oh, leven bucks an hour, eight hours, plus finish—that stuff ain't cheap, yuh know. How does two-hunnert sound?"

Self: "Sounds about typical. Try to get it done before the next administration comes in." (I turn to leave.)

M: "Jim-Bob, whats a 'nexudminustrashun?' "

Steve Smith

Low-House Seven

At my local gun club, the skeet shooters have a little saying that goes something like, "Nobody should miss a low-house seven." This refers to a target (clay) thrown by the trap located in the low house of a skeet field. The target emerges next to the shooter and proceeds straight away, the easiest of all shotgunning targets, and by far the easiest on the skeet field.

I got to thinking about this the other day while shooting with Al and Fritz and Bob and Mike (whose last names I'll withhold because they told their wives they were doing volunteer work at their churches) and was in the process of missing more than one low-house seven. There are lots of things in the outdoors that are low-house sevens, don't you agree? I mean, things that nobody should botch, but some of us manage to.

For example, everybody knows you don't get into a wood and canvas canoe while the thing is beached because your foot will go right through the canvas, right? Have you ever done that while a crowd was watching? Me too.

Or how about walking too close to a high bluff overlooking a quiet trout pool you plan to work and suffering what some refer to as 'clay bank surprise' whereby the participant crumbles the bank and enters the pool from an elevation of 100 feet and with the speed usually noted only in Olympic bobsled competitions.

Smile if you've ever pulled that one.

Also, everybody knows that you never hold a freshly landed lunker pike over the water to examine it and gloat a bit, because it just might slip back into the water and get off free, right? Heh, heh.

This little game of low-house seven is also the source of your odd yuk or two when it comes to turning the screws on your buddy every now and again. For example, let's say that the dog is locked up on a grouse during the early season when the vegetation is thick and visibility is nil. Since it's his shot, you sit back, light your pipe, and allow that the dog has the bird pinned so solid that only a fool would botch such a situation. "This is just like a low-house seven," you chuckle. Of course, Pal misses both barrels, and you and the dog sneer.

Or, maybe you offer advice from shore as he plays a nice steelhead into the shallows and mention that only a hamhanded so-and-so would manage to let the fish escape once it's that close, that it's so simple now that it's just like the famous LH7 situation. Whereupon the fish gives one of those patented steelhead tail flips and is gone posthaste, leaving buddy splattered with water and cussing and you're convulsed with laughter.

Try it, it's fun.

Steve Smith

Real
Outdoor Art

Where have all the artists gone? You know the ones, the people who have painted or drawn all those beautiful autumn hunting scenes for calendars, sporting magazines, and the like. Where are they when reality rears its ugly head during our outdoor pursuits? You've seen, I'm sure, the paintings of the two guys putting the finishing touches on their duck blind while the mallards, stacked up like jets over LaGuardia, wait patiently for the men to stop fussing around and get into the blind so they can pitch blindly into the decoys, offering shots seen only in paintings.

Where is the artist who will paint the real scene?

You are being trampled by a smelly, muddy Labrador retriever, the rain beating down on your bare head because you forgot your hat, while the ducks flare off at 200 yards because one of the blind's cattails was a little more brown than it should have been for that time of year.

Or in the grouse covers. The painted scene shows a blooded setter with a grouse nailed down tight next to one of those New England stone walls while the shooter, impeccably dressed, walks in—fine double gun held lightly but expertly. In the background, a flaming maple loses its scarlet leaves into a pristine, autumn blue sky.

For years, I figured that grouse only inhabited stone

walls, like the defenders of Tyre against the onslaught of Alexander's armies.

Where is the artist who will sketch the real scene?

Your dog busting a point that sets every grouse in the cover to wing. It doesn't matter though—the witch hazel and grapevines are so thick that you haven't touched the ground for the last 100 yards, and even if the birds went up in front of you, you couldn't see them. You probably couldn't hit them either, because the $80 pump gun you carry has been rusted tight by three weeks of rain during the season anyhow.

How about those heartwarming scenes in the traditional deer hunting camp on the evening of opening day? Wool-clad sportsmen, puffing fine briar pipes around a roaring fireplace, bunks neatly made and awaiting their weary bodies for the night. Outside, rolling fat bucks are hanging high, testifying to the skill of these paragons of the cedar swamps.

Where is it painted that you'll oversleep the first morning, walk 18 miles to a cold deer stand, sit for nine hours without blinking, watch one red squirrel and a flock of chickadees, and trudge home through the winter's first and worst blizzard?

And this one has got to be the worst: The painting of the fine belton setter, basking in a field of cut wheat stubble, a brace of pheasants lying near him along with a basket of pumpkins, apples, and other fall bounty—a few crimson leaves scattered about for effect.

In reality, our artist would capture on canvas the scene of either you or me wrestling the dog—which rolled in something dead about three hours ago—trying his level best to eat the birds lying near him while bruised apples and pumpkins with worms in them go rolling helter-skelter.

I guess wanting to finally find one of those idyllic scenes is what keeps us going back.

Steve Smith

The
Incomers

Well, it happened the other day. Seems I got caught. You know how it is. You get to talking with an acquaintance over the phone and you get to bragging about not only what a great shot you are, but also how your dog is flawlessly trained, your covers are teeming with grouse and woodcock and—for a little spice—throw in the fact that your daughter is also class valedictorian.

Not that you aren't to be believed. But the guy's like in Nebraska, so what's the harm in stretching the truth a tiny bit? I mean, he's never going to know, right?

Well, I was doing this the other day to a telephone friend of mine from the Great American Desert, a guy I've never met personally, but who I like anyway. I was spreading (spelled "shoveling") it sort of thick, and pretty soon he starts talking about his calendar, the opener in my home state, and the nearest available commercial airport. Being a big shot, I go along with the gag. Next thing I know, the date is set, he's coming, and it's put-up-or-shut-up time. Gulp.

Now, my pal-whom-I've-never-met is typical. He's an M.D. which means he's used to living like a Mideast potentate. He shoots a matched—that's MATCHED—set of Churchill doubles that he had built in England (after a trip there for that purpose), he has three crackerjack bird dogs (my dog is presently outside pointing flies on the patio), normally hunts in both Maine AND New Brunswick, and is not only younger than I am, he's also a jogger!

Now, right off, I know what you're thinking—why doesn't Smitty just get out of it? I can tell YOU'VE never been in this one before.

First off, I set myself up by being the greatest, to hear me tell it.

Secondly, I have the remnants of a reputation to maintain. Lastly, I don't know how. I can't lie my way out—fibbing got me here!

Not only does the guy have great dogs, he's shipping two ahead for several weeks of work on grouse by a pro trainer. (My dog has stopped pointing flies and is now eating the sofa.)

If you've ever had this happen, you know what's in store. The fella, being from out west where only (you should pardon) pheasants live, has long been enamored of grouse and woodcock hunting. He collects the best of grouse literature, limited edition grouse prints—if not the originals—and really wants to get into some birds.

Oh, I know, he talks about the "experience" and how bagging birds isn't important to him (if he isn't concerned about actually *shooting* the woodcock, he could hunt them in Nebraska). He talks about the sporting ethic and a prize well won after a fair chase. HA! You and I know he's coming here expecting to see grouse under every bracken fern and behind every tag alder. If there isn't, he'll be disappointed, and I'll be a philistine.

What should I do? That's the problem.

I thought, first of all, about getting him really bushed by taking him through a clearcut the first day. But, no good. The guy's a doctor and he jogs, which means he's in better shape than I am. I don't think the punishment for my lies should be death.

Next, I thought of admitting up front that I'm not that great and that I hope we'd find some birds, but dismissed this out of hand as being ridiculous.

I thought of trying my level best at showing him a good time but thought better of it. If he has a good time, he'll be back next year, and I'll be right up against it again.

No, I finally hit on it: I'll get the sucker lost. I mean, I'll get him sun-going-down, heart-in-the-mouth, I'll-never-see-Becky-and-the-kids-again *lost*. Naturally, I'll go get him later, but not until after I've scared his liver into Jello.

Now, how to do it—how to plot this heinous crime against a perfectly trusting sap like Doctor Jim?

Well, the answer to that was obvious; I'll take him hunting with Crazy Mortie. Crazy Mortie has gotten me lost so many times that even the Sheriff's Department has lost count.

Crazy Mortie is one of those maddening souls that always, but always, knows where he is in the woods. No compass. No map. No nuthin'. He just knows.

Now, trying to act like a real woodsman, I always try to pretend that I, too, am related to D. Boone and K. Carson. I also always end up turned around. It's quite simple, really, the way it happens.

Mortie, who doesn't speak all that clearly and is not a scholar of the communicative arts, gives directions to me before we enter one of his covers. He mumbles which way he'll go and which way I'll go, comments on the local terrain, and indicates what he'll have his nondescript setter doing. It sorta goes like this:

MORTIE: "Let's hunt this cov'r headin' west for about 40-50 rods 'n then cut south till we get 'crost t'tha big beaver dam if it's still there 'n if it ain't we'll go that way anyhow."

ME: "Mortie, which way's west?"

MORTIE: "After we cross th' swap me 'n th'e dog'll hit that li'l alder swale whilst you wait at the end 'cause there ain't nuff room for all us in th' swale 'n next we'll swing west again to 'rd what was onct the old Johnston place, 'cept the bank took it back in '54 or '55 and Old Man Johnston burned it down for spite. 'Course if there ain't no birds there we'll hafta work back south till we hit the third ridge, that's the li'l one 'bout four foot high—ain't but 70-80 rods from the old house place 'n there oughta be a bird sittin' 'long that ridge catchin' sun."

ME: "Mortie, is *that* the way west?"

MORTIE: "Anaway, that'll put us near the old tote road that the CCC boys cut back in '37 but ya gotta look good for it 'cause it's 'bout growed over 'n we'll take the road back thisaway till we git to the truck. Now, no talkin', no callin', 'n let's stay 'bout 10 rods apart. The stuff's thick, so try'n stay with me. Let's go."

ME: "You're really not going to tell me which way west is, are you Mortie?"

Yep, the more I think about it the more sure I am that Mortie and Doctor Jim are going to meet each other real soon.

Steve Smith

Why Not?

My personal philosophy in many areas has been the simplistic attitude of "why not?" Not only does this reflect a certain lack of serious thinking on my part, but it shows how lightly I regard future consequences. Ordering new guns, for example, shows that one forgets or ignores the fact that one will not have any more money to spend on guns in six months from now than one has in his pocket at the moment. One will, no doubt, have to go to the bank again and say he is building another new bathroom and acquire a home owner's loan. Another shameful experience (shameful is not exactly the right word as you will see) is coming downstairs on Saturday morning in your gunning clothes because you said "why not?" to some invitation and discovering the family all dressed up and waiting for you to take them to the zoo—because when they asked you about *that* you again said "why not?"

A man who is shortsighted enough to go around saying "why not?" like a parrot with the IQ of a clay target is also not the kind of guy who keeps any sort of engagement calendar. "Why not?" has resulted in my wife preparing a meal for eight when she expected three. And once in a while someone else has to drive me home, or put me up for the night, because they broke out the Virginia Gentlemen or Jack Daniels after dinner.

On the other, or positive, hand are the pleasures you

can have when you toss yourself on the seas like a bottle to find out where you'll turn up next. You remember the story of the man who in his final breaths called in his family and said "I must apologize to you all. I suppose I haven't been the perfect father and husband. I shamefully admit that I spent as much of my life as I could with the guns and the dogs. I was rarely at home during the hunting seasons and I'll admit that I spent too much time at the gun club." He paused here to rest for a minute, then continued. "I've been a terrible father and I hope you all forgive me." He paused again and looked around. Then he closed his eyes and smiled and said in a half-whisper to himself, "and on the other hand—I *have* shot a helluva lot of birds."

Gene Hill

The
Horseman

There was a short period of my life (called youth) when, except for Sunday school and baths, I lived in a cowboy outfit, including furry chaps, gloves, and real Western boots sent by my uncle from Oklahoma.

I finally outgrew my costume, and my dreams of becoming a cowboy (which were structured around visions of myself being always long, lean, tanned, and wearing just the right hat and boots) were sorely restricted in fulfillment by being brought up in an environment that featured an absence of steers and my own lively suspicions regarding the general intelligence and goodwill of horses.

But my respect for cowboys and Western guides remains as strong as ever. This is due partly to my envy of anyone who lives in such magnificant country, partly because of my constant amazement that these men can always make a horse go in the direction they want and make it stop when they want and partly because they seem to be the archetypical country men who can do anything and do it pretty well.

Fate, which usually leaves me drawing three cards to a low pair, for once turned the other cheek and got me mixed up with an outfitter named Cotton Gordon, from Lake George, Colorado.

Cotton is pretty close to the vision every kid had of himself as a cowboy; he and I hit it off right away and had a fine time discussing six million things about our coming

high-country hunt except one crucial point. It never occurred
to Cotton, who lives on a horse, that I have limited my
relationship to such animals to the occasional $2 bet or, at
most, watching the morning workouts at the August meeting
at Saratoga with an avaricious eye.

Cotton assumed that everyone knew something, however slight, about riding. I assumed that we would arrive in
camp by a method that didn't feature horses. We were both
wrong.

The full impact of what lay in store didn't hit until I
found myself staring at a string of horses being saddled and
packed and heard one of Cotton's hands asking me to walk
around and pick out a horse. I laughed and asked him if any
of the horses happened to be named Old Maude, Lazybones,
or anything similar that was descriptive of old age, docility,
or maidenly virtue. He said no, all the horses were pretty
good; Cotton wasn't one of the type that tolerated anything
but good horseflesh. I asked him, "Pretty good for what?
Casey Tibbs?" He laughed again and pointed to a pile of
saddles. He told me to pick one out, with the air of one fine
judge of things horsey confiding to another, then went about
his work of loading the pack animals.

I took about the same enthusiastic pleasure in choosing
a horse and saddle as I would in choosing a time bomb. So
I did what any sensible man would do—nothing. I decided
to put my faith in luck and Cotton Gordon. And I was right.
Cotton saddled up Sundown, a middle-aged, pleasant-gaited,
and even-tempered mare, and led us down the trail that
wound toward camp. The ride itself was fine. The weather
was perfect, and from the top of the mesa we could see the
green river valleys below and the snow-capped mountains
above. The Colorado air was a bouquet of late autumn, and
now and then we could see mule deer watching us pass from
the edge of the aspens.

The old mare and I were getting along famously. After
an hour or so of timid and questioning indoctrination, our
relationship solidified, and I began to believe I was one of
those few that were born to horseback. Sundown and I would

canter frivolously for a few minutes to catch up with the rest of the group. (Lest you share the same question about the name Sundown that I did, it referred to her reddish sunset coloration and not the more ominous overtones that leapt instantly to my morbid mind.)

I won't say I wasn't relieved to finally see the tents in the distance, but the ride had caused little discomfort in those parts featured in cartoons about beginning horsemen, and my practice turns and changes of gear were beginning to show some results, and I felt that Sundown and I had established a good, basic, master/servant relationship.

Cotton from time to time had ridden back to chat and see how I was getting along, and while I won't say he was visibly impressed, he was at least obviously relieved to note that I hadn't fallen off or suffered some other catastrophe. We both felt at the close of our journey that my riding worries were over. We were, again, both wrong.

I arrived at the hitching rail dead last. Some were casually unsaddling their horses; others had already finished and were in their tents unpacking or standing around admiring the view. Cotton was supervising the unloading of the pack horses, organizing the beginnings of supper, seeing to it that everyone was comfortable, telling funny stories, and managing to be involved in doing nine or ten things at the same time and doing them all well. I was still on Sundown, who had forgotten me and wandered off into the meadow to graze. I was trying to look as casual as I could—as if the whole scene were purposeful, the faithful steed feeding quietly under the quiet control of her benevolent master.

"Going to join us for supper in the tent or shall I arrange to have you fed up there?" Cotton had finally diagnosed the situation and was standing looking up at me with a quiet smile. "Some folks take to riding right off and can't get enough of it," he went on, "but you sure are one of the most dedicated I've ever seen!"

"Cotton," I whispered, "I can't get off."

"What do you mean you can't get off?" he said in a voice

laden with disbelief. "You don't know how—or you don't want to?"

"I want to get off about as much as anything I ever wanted in my life," I told him, "but I can't move my right leg. I can't throw it over the saddle."

"Well then, can you move your left leg and get off the other side? I hate to have to shoot old Sundown just to get you on the ground."

The fact that a horse has two sides had never occurred to me, and while Cotton held the horse still, I slid off and began hobbling around. When he finished tying her up and removing the tack he asked me how I felt.

"Fine," I told him, "must have been a little catch in a muscle."

Cotton went on to tell me how even the most experienced riders sometimes got a little catch like that, but I'd be fine tomorrow. And after Cotton's steak supper, I took a little walk and went over to see Sundown for a chat. To my surprise, I did feel fine.

Cotton's the kind of outfitter who runs a happy camp. He's a good cook, and a nonstop storyteller who only pauses long enough to laugh at a tale of yours. So by bedtime, I'd nearly forgotten the fact that I had an early morning date with Sundown. My mind was on mule deer and trying to remember a good story to top one Cotton had broken up the camp with. But the next morning found the kid who liked to play cowboy all played out.

From where I sat resting my leg, I could look out over the little brook that ran through the foot of the camp and see the great West repeating itself—mountain after mountain separated by vast meadows and low woodlands.

In the distance across the valley some of our pack horses were working out their own kinks, rolling in the soft meadow grass like so many russet puppies. I could hear them playing and could imagine the men that first tamed this massive country sitting, in times past, around a camp a bit like mine and thinking not in terms of distance that they had to travel but in terms of time—weeks and months that spread out between Denver and some tiny ranch house they might call home.

I remembered their lonesome songs created to help pretend they had a name other than Pete or Red and friends who knew it.

I thought I'd just sit there for a morning, keep the fire working, rest my leg and think. Maybe the West will grow a little smaller for me as time goes by. I'd like to get comfortable with this country, but a man has to grow into it— he has to learn to sing the lonesome songs before this kind of country looks like home.

Gene Hill

The
Christmas Card
Letter

Do you remember not too long ago when the Christmas Card Letter was in vogue? You know, the letter that went out with the card and said stuff like: "Johnathan is teaching evenings at the University while still keeping up his thriving law practice. Jennifer, having graduated as valedictorian from high school, is now majoring in psychology at Cornell and has, for the first semester, kept her traditional four-point. Meanwhile, Jeffery—our baby—has started his own thriving carpet-cleaning business and expects to gross $74,000 next year as a high school sophomore." Ad nauseum.

People have pretty much stopped sending those things because they generally either took a lot of flack about them, ran out of lies to tell, or stopped having enough friends to make the investment at Quick Print worthwhile.

Well, *not me*. Here's the one I sent out last year. In case you missed it, read on:

Dear _____

Well, another year has gone by; they seem to do that with regularity. And, since this is the holiday season, I thought I'd jot you a line about what's going on at my place so that you could get your usual early winter yuks at my expense.

Last year started innocently enough. I planned a little bone fishing off the Keys in January, with maybe some tarpon fishing as an aside. What I didn't know is that my leathery old skin wasn't as leathery as I thought. I found out that I went from get-off-the-airplane directly to sunstroke. I didn't tan, get pink, pass Go, collect $200. Nothing. I went from Michigan white to the hospital. I didn't think the bottoms of your feet could peel, but—by God—they can. So much for the January trip.

February marked the usual midwinter steelhead fishing trip that I look forward to each year. This time, things didn't work out exactly as I'd planned. I had a nice fish on—probably a 12-pounder—when a damn whistle started to blow. I didn't pay much attention to it because the fish was making a long run right then. The roar of water upriver sort of made me take notice, though. I sure wish they'd give you a decent warning before they opened the dam, something like: "HEY YOU, SMITH! WE'RE GONNA OPEN THE DAM!" Well, they don't and I hadda be fished out of the river by the water patrolmen (see enclosed wire-service clipping).

March was pretty uneventful except that my kid brother, Eric, talked me into our annual ice-fishing trip on Lake Huron. Just like last year, he talked me into it on the day the ice decided to break up after laying there for six months. Yeah, the Coast Guard again. (see wire service clipping #2, enc.).

April, when the trout season opened, was a good month. I caught a few nice fish—some even on flies! And, except for mistaking a poisonous mushroom for a morel and getting my stomach pumped out, it wasn't too bad.

Nothin' much happened in May.

June was a toughie. That nice quiet little river (the nameless one I told you about last year) sprouted a goddam canoe livery this year, complete with college kids. They sure got a few laughs at my expense from splashing and diving in the pool I was working. Going fishing on Wednesdays didn't even help. What DID help was the 80-pound test mono strung neck-high across the stream. They got wet, *I* got the laughs.

July. That's when I did the 30 days for assault you all heard about (see June, above).

August was spent dog training my new setter pup, Jess.

Bloodlines better than mine, and certainly better than Tom McGarrity, the guy I got her from.

Well, anyhow, my dog training skills being what they are, she has turned out about the way you'd expect. So far, she hasn't pointed anything, ate the neighbor's pet chinchilla, and lives better than I do. I should have known something was going to screw up my grouse season, but in August, you're always hopeful.

September. The grouse and woodcock opener. Boyoboyoboy. The rain we had made my favorite covers a swamp. One cover that IS a swamp anyway was impassible. I know it was impassible because I tried passing through in my Jeep. The enclosed clipping #3 tells it all. That's me standing next to the roof of the Jeep. That's all that shows after I hit the quicksand bog. I don't know *whereinhell* all those people and the photographer came from.

September was also the month that a doctor friend of mine came in to hunt. He tells me beforehand that he wants good dog work and a chance to be away from his practice. He rolls in, gets out of the car, and tells me he came to kill birds—to hell with the dog work. Doing the natural thing, I got him lost. I didn't plan on losing him for three days, though. He left right after we found him.

October was a good month. I finally got my gun back from Jim Bob the gunsmith after eight months and I had some good dog work as Jess blundered into a few birds. I took my usual season's quota of three grouse and two woodcock with three boxes of shells. The 20 gauge with the extra weight and the longer barrels helped a lot. I got slickered into a fall fishing trip for pike which didn't turn out too well. Crazy Charlie got hit by lightning. I got into a disagreement with a bow hunter who got mad because I was hunting while he was trying to act like a goddam Indian. Nothing much happened. His hair stood up and he walked around stiff-legged for a bit, but he calmed down once I paid him the 20 bucks.

November was bad for me, gang. I got talked into going pheasant hunting in Iowa for a week. Out there, they can have a blizzard anytime after the third of June, and they had one the day I arrived. Played gin rummy for five days and lost every cent I had plus three boxes of high-brass 6's to Dave Meisner. Saw two pheasants—both road kills —on the way home.

December. Outside of mailing this letter, I haven't gone outside all month, nor do I plan to. Oops. Forgot. I had to go outside to help the firemen when I had that chimney fire. Didn't get my wood in on time and it was green, and. . .hell, you know.

Anyway, have a nice holiday.

Pray for me.
Smitty

Steve Smith

The Perfect Woman

I try to spend a few days goose shooting in Easton, Maryland, every year with David Crosby, an old friend of mine. Crosby is one of the best wing shots and skeet shooters in our area—good enough to have the gall to occasionally show up at a registered shoot wearing linen plus fours. In an effort to do something about the local laundry situation, Crosby married. During what turned out to be an eight-hour lull in the shooting, I asked Crosby if his bride, Barbara, was surprised when she received a shotshell reloader for Christmas, when I knew she was expecting a vacuum cleaner. Crosby said he'd be glad to buy her a new vacuum cleaner when they made one that would also turn out 200 12-gauge skeet loads an hour.

We got to discussing wives, and George Martin, who was also sleeping in the blind with us, mentioned that a friend of his had discovered the perfect woman. "And what's perfect?" I asked him.

George smiled wistfully and said, "For me, about 14½ in length of pull, 1⅜ at the comb and 2 inches drop at heel."

Gene Hill

Of Dogs and Men

In case you haven't noticed, there are basically two types of gun dogs in this world—ours and the other guy's. This is not a mere fact of ownership, but is more a fact of behavior and training. Ours are usually not to be mentioned in the same breath with champion bloodlines, well mannered field decorum, or even good looks, generally.

In point of fact, the comparison is usually easy to make because while the Other Guy's Dog is diligently searching out game, has a covey of quail pinned down, or has nailed an old rooster grouse by a picturesque New England stone wall, our mutt is off by himself doing something associated with juvenile delinquency in humans.

Have you ever noticed that the difference between our dog and the Other Guy's Dog shows up right away on a hunt? If you and the Other Guy are planning a hunt together, and you agree to drive, when you stop at his house to pick him up, his dog is sedately on the front steps, keeping company with the gear the man has set outside awaiting your arrival. When you open the door for the other man, YOUR dog bounds out, crosses the street, and commences opening the neighbor's trash bags that have been thoughtfully provided for his investigation.

As you drive to the shooting grounds, the Other Guy's Dog waits in quiet anticipation, perhaps catching a quick snooze against the coming exertion of hunting. Our mutt?

He is eating the upholstery on the back seat. Of course, this doesn't agree with his delicate gastronomical system, so he takes care of that in short order by throwing up all over the place.

I once owned a beautiful golden retriever. She was an instant motion sickness case whenever she took a car trip. Put her in the car, turn on the ignition, and she got a little green around the gills. Back out of the driveway, and it was strange, strangling sounds from the rear seat. Go around the block and mister, you had a cleanup job to do. This was the same dog that could eat raw fish heads without a belch.

Arriving at the first cover of the day, you'll notice that the Other Guy's Dog will quarter the cover nicely, always turning outward on the turns at the end of each sweep. What does our dog do? Runs as fast as possible in a straight line toward the horizon. The route she has taken can be traced by the sounds of grouse flushing and an occasional yap of delight eminating from the cur.

Once a bird has been located, the Other Guy's Dog will pin it down every time. Our dog simply loves to point. I once hunted with a dog that could point like none I've ever seen. In one day, this specimen pointed three woodcock, five grouse, a rooster pheasant, two rabbits, a flock of juncos down from the north, a discarded tractor tire, and a 1954 Chevy that had been stripped for parts.

Once a bird is down, our dog usually remembers that her stomach is empty because of earlier car sickness and will promptly eat the first bird of the day—head, bill, and feet included. How dogs can do this on a dead run with me chasing her, I'll never live long enough to learn, but they can.

Among the other things the dog who lives at our place can usually do on a typical day are: chase the chickens belonging to the farmer we are about to ask permission from to hunt on his acreage; incite to riot a heard of shorthorn cattle and the herd bull; roll in a three-week-old, road-killed raccoon; attempt copulation with the female bluetick hound that lives two miles away; pick a fight with a farm collie; take time out from the walk back to the car in order to take a mudbath in a drainage ditch; eat our lunches; lose the collar and the bell and then lose the spare collar and bell; run some deer for a bit, and manage to get tangled up with any of the following: a porcupine, a skunk, a she-bear with half-grown cubs, or an electric fence.

About the time that we are figuring out if the route home will take us by the local dog pound, the mutt slaps into a classic point. You walk in, expecting a woodchuck or something equally exotic, and out bursts two grouse. You are so surprised that you down both with snappy right and left barrels. The dog retrieves each perfectly, and you are euphoric.

As you arrive home, after singing the dog's praises over the miles, Fang exits the car and evacuates on the wife's prime rosebushes before taking time to rip up the evening paper. Ah well, at least he's ours.

If the behavior of our dog is reprehensible, what can be said of the training methods we used to mold this animal into its present form? In other words, where did we goof? Maybe it was by allowing the dog to think of itself as people. Have you ever noticed that? How come some mutts seem to think they are actually living and breathing examples of genus *Homo*, species *sapien?* You know the routine. A pal stops over to sample a little hard cider and talk ducking or grouse hunting or prospects for the upcoming pheasant opener. What happens? Fido slides right in beside you, pours himself a glass of spirits, drapes his arm around your shoulder, and enters into the conversation in low whines and an odd growl or two here and there.

Your pal, the guy with the well-trained dog, looks at you like you've got two heads for allowing this. You and I will, on this occasion, remark that the dog is very friendly, that the dog likes human company, or that the dog likes the smell of woodsmoke from the fireplace and the odor of Hoppes No. 9. What we don't remark is that the dog doesn't consider himself a dog—hasn't been for months, as far as he can recollect.

In field training, we substitute words like "aggressive"

when we mean unbiddable, "self thinker" when we mean boneheaded, and "good nose" when he can wind the neighbor's in-season poodle at 200 yards. In other words, we allow behavior in our dogs we'd never allow in our kids or wives.

Since we are usually inept with a smoothbore, most days, we stand for inept points. Maybe we secretly hope the mutt is kidding and we won't have to shoot and make collective fools of ourselves. If we do connect, the dog may try to eat the bird. Here is where some forceful training is necesasry.

A bird that has been force-fed to a bird-eating scalawag will cure the mutt of this little trick about 50 percent of the time. (The other 50 percent love it and ask for more.) Anyhow, grasping the dog securely by the collar, force the bird down his throat as far as possible. Don't be put off by the sounds of stomach gurgling, retching, dry heaves, and strangling noises. That's just you. It isn't nearly so hard on the dog.

A dog that ranges too far out can quickly be cured of this fault by wedging a forepaw under his collar. The dog must now operate on three legs, which cuts down on the monkeyshines about 25 percent. A buddy of mine pulls this on his dog when the animal is especially frisky. By the time he gets hold of the dog, the mutt is sitting serenely, with the about-to-be-imprisoned paw raised and ready for incarceration. All he's done so far is train the fastest three-legged setter in the state.

When I was a kid, I can remember one vivid experience having to do with slowing down a fast-moving bird dog. A few minutes before legal shooting time, I saw a pickup truck come barreling down a dirt road at about 30 miles an hour. In the back of the truck, a man stood, holding a rope connected to a pointer trotting alongside the vehicle. I remember the holder of the rope shouting above the sound of the engine:

"Faster, he ain't even tired yet and season opens in five minutes!" When I sw that party later, my dad asked them about their dog—noticeable by his absence. "Aw, hell. He took off 40 rods when we untied his rope and we ain't seen 'im since. Prob'ly won't till dark." So much for the tire-them-out routine.

Speaking of bad habits, I once knew a dog that had an absolute fetish for trying to catch and kill a creature that we state of Washington kids called mountain beaver. I know, now, that these animals were the common marmots, or 'whistle pigs' of the Rockies. Well, old Duke would saunter off into the back country and listen to those marmots whistling to each other. Pretty quick, he couldn't stand it anymore and he'd take off after one.

Now I always kind of figured that this is what the marmots wanted, because they'd gang up on old Duke and beat him to a bloody pulp. He'd finally break off battle and retreat for the safety of his warm box in the utility room of a friend of mine, his owner. He'd lay around for three or four days and convince himself he wasn't dead, then it was off for another go 'round with the marmots. Duke never did win one, as far as we could tell, but he kept trying. There ought to be a message there, but it escapes me.

Another mutt of my acquaintance was a pointer with tastes that leaned toward bologna sandwiches. She wouldn't budge from the car for the first cover of the day until she'd downed at least one bologna sandwich, and with lots of mustard, too. None of your peanut butter and jelly, either. It was bologna or here I stay.

Still another couldn't resist chasing chipmunks. She'd hunt just fine until we crossed a hot chipmunk track. Then, all normal functions ceased and it was Katie-bar-the-door. She'd take off howling like a beagle until she'd either treed, holed up, or reduced to possession the offending rodent. When she did catch one, she invariably brought it back alive for inspection, whereupon her owner would curse her roundly and release the hapless little beast. From the sounds of things, the chipmunk enjoyed this about as much as I'd enjoy being my own dentist. I don't speak chipmunk, and I was often glad of it. The dog was nearly perfect in all other details, yet she never lost this urge and was indeed, chasing chipmunks when she was past 11 years of age. She never caught very many at that age, by the way.

I guess the point of all of this is that dogs are a fact of life. Like women, taxes, and an occasional pull from a jug of our favorite beverage, we can't live with them, or indeed without them.

Steve Smith

The
Duck Hunter

My pal Crazy Charlie is a duck hunter. Now, besides you and me, nobody else knows I associate with the character. I mean, a visit to his place is like a journey back in time to another place, the era of the great hordes of ducks over the Chesapeake and the Susquehanna. Real, old time, Down East waterfowling is alive and well at Charlie's place.

Now, I don't mind an outdoor decor. In fact, what passes for my den-office-hunting lodge-rattrap is furnished in early ruffed grouse. But Charlie has taken a good thing a bit too far.

For example, the first thing you notice when you walk into the house is the smell. Not disagreeable mind you, just different than what you come to expect houses to smell like. It took me a few visits to figure it out, but I finally did. Charlie's place—the whole bloody house—smells like a wet Lab.

Somehow, he has been able to capture the essence of that singular odor and it is part of the heating/cooling system in his home. Certainly, the smell could come from the three large, black Labs that are draped, like so many tapestries, over the furniture and on the carpets. These mutts are not what you would call obedience champs. They pretty much do what they want. A visitor to the house is treated to a couple good, smart whacks in the chops by one of those two-pound tails every trip. Charlie likes this because this reminds him of when he's hunting, and the Labs take turns beating a tattoo on his bridgework all day long.

Besides the usual stuff you'd expect in the home of a known waterfowler—David Maass prints of ducks and geese, old decoys, mounted ducks, photos of old dogs and old gunning companions, stacks of *Waterfowler's World Magazine,* and a few empty shells set about commemorating some feat of wingshooting skill (most likely luck)—Crazy Charlie has added a few new wrinkles.

For instance, his downstairs den is carpeted with a rug that has the pattern of muddy dog footprints woven into the fabric. This way, Charlie's sainted wife, Sharon, doesn't have to worry about how the place looks—not that she ever, by choice, goes down there.

And, when you walk into the den, you are greeted at the doorway by a blast of arcticlike air that Charlie pipes in. Unless he is on the verge of hypothermia most of the time, he just doesn't feel right.

Instead of a coffee table, he's got an old canoe turned over so the bottom is up. That vessel has a hole in the bottom placed there by an errant charge of chilled four's. If you are smart, you will never—but never—ask Charlie how the boat got in that condition.

Charlie's kids are models of decorum. They respond to hand signals, they "come," "sit," and "stay" upon command. Jeff, the younger of the two, is still having a little trouble with "get back," but he's coming along nicely. Charlie hopes to have him finished by the time the kid hits kindergarten.

Dinner at Charlie's place is a real experience. Sweetwife and I got invited over for the first time the other night, and I was really ready for braized mallard or even roast Canada goose.

Ha.

We arrive, have a drink (served from a Thermos painted, not too neatly, olive drab—"OD green" in the parlance), and talk about the weather conditions on the Canadian prairies.

Charlie shows me his Ducks Unlimited donor stickers and his latest issue of *Gun Dog*. Sweetwife looks at me as tears of boredom start to well up in her eyes.

Finally, the long-suffering Sharon tells us that dinner is ready. We sit down at the dining room table (I had never before seen chairs with oarlocks) and the meal is brought on.

Instead of the anticipated goodies, we have placed before us a wet lunch bag, complete with Lab teeth marks. Inside the bag, there is a jelly sandwich, a wilted pickle, three stale and somewhat soggy cookies, and an apple that had seen its best days sometime during the Truman administration. A typical waterfowler's lunch. Charlie dives in with relish. I start looking for the potted palm.

After dinner, we again hit the Thermos. This time, I hit it with dead seriousness. The evening's entertainment consists of listening to Charlie and his Olt do the feeding chuckle, an 8mm home movie presentation of flighting waterfowl with identification required by all viewers, and inspection of the stock work on his pet Remington 1100 magnum.

Finally, Charlie looks out the window and notices that the sun is below the horizon. Naturally, when he comments on this, I figure we're going to really get serious about the Thermos. Nope. Instead, Charlie stands, tells us thanks for coming, and shows us the door.

Walking toward the car, it occurs to me what had happened. It was sundown—the end of legal shooting time. Charlie didn't know what to do with us, so he just picked up and we left.

If you are interested in meeting Charlie, just drop me a line. I'm sure he'd like to meet you. After all, he's a little short of friends right now.

Steve Smith

Acting Rich

Sooner or later, most of us discover that there are, unfortunately, no great-aunts or uncles who are determined to name us their favorite relative. We also know too well, that daily labor at our appointed tasks hardly keeps us even, and we have only the magic of the Irish Sweepstakes or the like to come and pluck us from our struggle in financial quicksand and swoop us to the heady peaks of affluence.

I am always horribly disappointed to read in the paper about some guy who hits the big one and is photographed holding a check that represents $50,000 a year for life. He is more than likely to say, "I don't think this will change our way of life too much. Barbara and I will put the money in the bank, and I guess I'll just stay on doing what I'm doing." Well, you can bet your leather-topped rubbers that it would sure change my life! I am not in the habit of banking money, and I do not intend to start now. And as for continuing to work every day, an attitude like that could give the whole gambling thing a bad name.

But should this be the year that the Telegram arrives from Dublin, are you ready? Have you been practicing that different tone of voice that wealth entitles you to? Will you ever send back an overdone sirloin to the chef? Have you ever refused to tip a nasty, inefficient waiter? Why not start now?

Take, for example, the following letter. Save it if you

like. It can be used as a form to follow for tone of voice, attitude, etc. I have, of course, written others in order to have them ready—to my gunmakers, my plantation overseer, and my private pilot. But, this will do to start off.

Messrs._____,Tailors
00 Savile Row, London, England

My Dear Sirs:
The three shooting suits ordered on the 16th inst. have arrived—quite tardy as usual. Your constant refusal to use more than a few pennies for postage has ensured that the package has journeyed to the United States via Tasmania, Borneo, and Guam. At the prices you are charging me, I was led to expect hand delivery via Royal Messenger. My disappointment at the condition of the garments is only matched by my complete disbelief that you actually measured me when I was in London following my last shoot at my estate in Scotland.

It is, of course, remotely possible that you do have another customer named Gene Hill who is apparently in the employ of a European circus as the lead dwarf. The tightness of the sleeves in the dun-colored, unfinished worsted could lead to severe circulatory problems, were it not for the fact that the breadth across the shoulders is so scant that it is impossible for me to wear the jacket more than five minutes at a time without requiring assistance from my valet in disrobing.

The beige, covert-cloth model with the Campbell tartan lining is a comparable masterpiece. I was actually able to put it on without assistance and was very nearly able to button the front.

I immediately took up my favorite Churchill (the one with the 25-inch barrels I mentioned to you) and swung as if at a crossing bird. The resultant ripping sound so startled my man Baldwin that he nearly let the Purdey I was preparing to try next drop from his gloved hands. I was fully prepared to shred the garment in anger but you had foreseen that, I'm sure, by so constructing it that it fell apart, panel by panel, before I could do any real violence to the material.

As for the shepherd's check of which I was so especially fond, I have given it to Baldwin, who, you may recall, is constructed along the lines of a Bartlett pear, and who carries himself with a curious stooping list, most of which is due to a legendary affection for the grape. However, the poor wretch is pleased with the garment as it fits him perfectly. I have deducted half of its cost from his wages and he talks constantly of my generosity. I do not expect you to try to extort payment from me for the other half if you value our long relationship. Along with the two suits I am returning, you will find a blue denim jacket that I am enclosing for size; please return this with the two suits as I still occasionally shoot quail with my relatives.

I am most pleased with the neckties, both in fit and cut. I'm sure that the only reason we don't have them that narrow over here is that the bootlace companies would object to unfair competition.

My solicitors in London, Navin & Openshaw, assure me that my case against you for misrepresentation will be eagerly received in your courts should I not be in receipt of the above garments within 90 days.

Most cordially,
Gene Hill

Gene Hill

August

Patrick McManus once wrote that he thought God had made March in case eternity proved too short. Well, I agree with Pat, but personally offer August as my month of 200 days. August, the month before some hunting seasons open, is pure, blue murder on the nerves.

August tempts you. A few cool nights, some early morning fog, nearly full grown grouse chicks running across a country road. Honestly, it's enough to make you cry.

To combat August, lots of people do strange things. Some men work their dogs to a trembling froth. Others bother their wives to a trembling froth. At my house, the August doldrums bring about a strange situation. I, for my part, look forward to the fall and the sports it brings—primarily grouse and woodcock hunting. Sweetwife, my life's mate, thinks in terms of cleaning up the house, catching up on the odd jobs, and generally making my life miserable for about a month until the first hunting season opens and she won't see me until Christmas.

I think this harkens back to Neanderthal times when the female started thinking of cleaning the odd bones, skins, and charred wood from the family cave once the days grew shorter. It must certainly be linked to the double X chromosome structure possessed by females, because no fella of my acquaintance is similarly moved.

Anyhow, the other day, right around August 1, Sweetwife stepped into what passes for my office-hunting lodge-inner-sanctum—she lovingly refers to it as "the Rattrap"—and started making noises about how I'd ought to clean out the CLOSET.

Now, I'm sure you have a CLOSET. This is where all the various and assorted trash you've accumulated over the years get stuffed. If you're like me, you know within six feet of where everything is in your closet, and you can put your hands on any of your sporting equipment with a minimum of confusion and profanity.

Sweetwife doesn't see it that way. I explained that the closet had a door and since I was the only one who went inside it, what was the big deal? Sweetwife gave me that look she gives me when her father wants to talk about politics with me, and I knew that I'd best keep quiet. Clearly, more drastic measures were needed.

I politely asked her if she would consider giving me a hand with the CLOSET, since a career of hunting was accumulated within its hallowed walls, and she agreed. The first thing I pulled from the closet was a handful of grouse tail feathers, dusty with age, from each grouse I'd shot during the last three or four seasons. Some of the feathers appeared to have been gnawed on a bit by some small mammal, and I pointed this out to the little woman. She started to look a little pale.

Next, the closet disgorged a series of mason jars, each containing the crop contents from grouse I'd shot and cleaned. At one time, I was going to prove that grouse eat different foods in odd numbered years or something equally ridiculous. Anyhow, jars labeled 1975, 1976, 1977, and 1978 emerged with their shriveled and wrinkled contents of berries, grapes, and green leaves. Sweetwife started to look a little green herself.

Next came my collection of rabbit skins. Some of these were a bit musty, and some were serving as condominiums for a lice population. I pleaded that it wasn't fair to toss these out as eviction went against my Midwest upbringing. Sweetwife's left eyelid started to twitch.

Finally, I dragged out an aspen log that had been gnawed on by a beaver. My three kids and I had picked it up on one of the trips afield we take so often when we all should be home being domestic. This particular log showed signs of hosting some wood beetles because it started to crumble in my hands. I turned to explain this phenomenon to the Storm and Strife only to see the door close behind her.

I chuckled to myself and reflected on male superiority. But, strangely, I was drawn to the closet. I investigated deeper. I found a spent 20-gauge shell tucked on a back shelf. It was the first one I'd ever fired from my brand new hand-me-down single barrel shotgun when I was 12. I remember Dad setting a tin can on a fence post and telling me to have at it. I remembered the trembling attempt to hold the barrel steady, to look cool and confident, and I remember the sharp jab of the 20's stock into my face and shoulder. That gun was built for someone with the face configuration of a Yorkshire hog, and I never could hit anything with it, but I never loved any gun more.

Next, I found the tail feather from a rooster pheasant, the first ringneck I'd ever seen shot. My Dad dropped it with a 45-yard crossing shot, and it seemed we had to run forever to get to the downed bird. His smooth old Model 12 had done the trick, though, and the bird lay still in the knee-high grass. We had no dog in those days. Old Champ, Dad's English setter had gone to wherever good bird dogs go, and I know now that the pain was still too great back then for Dad to replace him with another, lesser dog.

I dug a little deeper and found a yellowed black and white photo of my pal, Mark Sutton, and me with Tracy—about the finest Brittany I'd ever hunted behind. She wasn't my dog, but Mark's, but she loved me in her own way as I loved her. To her, I was October—her life. When I showed up at the farm, it was bird season, and she came alive when she saw me pull into the driveway. That picture was especially touching because it was less than two months later, during a Michigan blizzard, that Mark called to tell me she'd died of Parvo and the vet couldn't save her. Mark and I hunted together little the next season, and no dog yet has worn her bell, even though Mark has had other, maybe better dogs.

I reached into the back shelf of the closet and found another photo, this one of my own son, Chris, holding a big rooster grouse I'd shot on his first tag-along hunting trip. The look on his face was the same as I must have had on mine as I toted that long ago pheasant Dad had shot and I'd carried home. That look is the look of a convert—one who's hooked for life.

As I silently stowed the things back in the closet, I thought a bit on the shooting man's closet. If yours is like mine, the essence of your life is there.

Gene Hill

Fishing
Stronger Waters

Some years ago a major magazine published a cartoon showing two ardent outdoorsmen in a boat. One was saying, as he uncorked a bottle, "Beer's all right for trout, but for pike and bass—give me a nice, light ale!"

My first reaction was a laugh. My second—the feeling we've all shared—was that there is great truth in humor. The only thing dry about most fishing is a certain type of artificial lure. So I believe that we should make a study of what is the most appropriate beverage to imbibe while angling for certain species of fish.

The problem is not simple for the reason that there are more types of fish than types of alcoholic refreshements. We must, therefore, categorize according to the size of the fish sought, where it's taken (stream, lake, ocean, river, and so on) and the general climatic conditions that prevail. We will attempt to equate the sporting qualities of the fish and its locale with common and necessary tonic beverages.

Let me begin by saying that I don't think beer (or ale) should enter into it. There should *always* be beer, unless the temperature, such as often occurs while ice fishing, is below the freezing point. Beer is as necessary for giant tuna as it is to the quiet worm-dunker, half asleep in the sun, hoping, not very hard, to pick up a few crappies to prove to his wife that he really was fishing for the good of the family larder, not just out to have a splendid time by himself—an attitude all women violently oppose.

Nor are we discussing what you should have back at the camp or the cabin or stuck off somewhere in the boat. We are referring to the niceties of liquid refreshment that a man can and should carry on his person or as part of his regular equipment. In short, gentlemen, we speak of that noble instrument the FLASK. For those who are needy of potions requiring a high or low temperature, we will later propound the advantages of the short Thermos.

The flask should carry your initials and those of your next of kin in case of accident—or worse, loss of the flask. If you favor spinning tackle, trolling equipment or any sort of inexpensive glass rod, the modern (and unbreakable) polyethylene flask is good enough. If you are a purist favoring dry flies, Orvis rods, and multi-pocketed tailored wading jackets, you are in a position that necessitates the carrying of a nickel, silver, or pewter container.

If you favor bass plugging after dark, your flask should have a luminous paint finish and some kind of flotation should it be dropped overboard. If you are a "still fisherman" of the 25 cent bamboo-pole-and-string variety, I'm sure you have long since chosen the proper Mason jar, and have carefully protected it with several wrappings of friction tape.

As you can see, I am making the tacit recommendation that you have a "wardrobe" of flasks so that you may suit the flask to the fishing. There is nothing more distastefully showy than a man deep-trolling with a hand line (probably with a live frog and a June bug spinner) and flashing an engraved silver warmer.

Almost as bad, but not quite, is a correspondent of mine, one E. Schwiebert of New Jersey, who so favors handmade bamboo rods of the ounce-and-a-half persuasion that his flask has been veneered with simulated wickerwork and tasseled in the basic colors of a Royal Coachman. One affectation is as bad as the other.

Another bad example of the showy is a wealthy playboy,

E.Z. of Scarsdale, who has had made at considerable expense, hand-fitted flask covers in various plaids to match a variety of fishing shirts.

But, as important as the flask is, it must remain secondary to the selection of what fills it. This may be best explained by example: If I were, for illustration, fishing for salmon in Norway I would carry a silver flask filled with aquavit. Or on the Miramichee in New Brunswick, a pewter flask brimming with an eight-year-old Canadian rye. Another: smallmouths in the Rangeley Lakes of Maine (using a $5\frac{1}{2}$-foot plug rod of bamboo) require a gallon jug of 1959 hard cider.

See how simple it is when given a little thought? But it can get tricky. Imagine being invited to try a private beat for salmon in northern Britain. You guess a fine dry sherry? Wrong. Here it depends on the size of the fish. Sherry is fine for trout, but for grilse you must stay with an 86 proof scotch.

In America, it's really simple, disregarding the local exceptions that we cannot go into here. For stream fishing (I assume for trout) we like to stay with applejack, or scotch if you're east of the Mississippi River (with the exception of Pennsylvania, where it is preferred to offer rye).

When lake fishing—and we can pretty much disregard the size of the fish since the majority of fishermen do likewise—I like to stay with brandy when the weather's cold and favor a red wine when summer comes.

Speaking of hot and cold brings us to the vacuum bottle. Again it isn't too difficult for our common sense to see us through: whiskey sours, john collins, and toddies when the weather is chilly or we are on the lake. For warm weather or stream fishing, gin slings, rum and tonic, or a nicely chilled white wine soda will see us through without disgrace; these also do very nicely on salt water, and are especially well received amid a nice run of blues or fluke.

This, gentlemen, I consider just a basic primer and it is done in answer to many requests. Local options make really sweeping generalizations impossible. If, for example, you plan a sturgeon jaunt along the Snake, or a week afloat on the Arkansas, I will answer you according to your specific needs.

You may have noticed I have neglected to mention the martini. One cannot really limit the use of the martini or presume to dictate when or where it cannot be taken. I once advised a Mr. Cornelius Ryan to carry his martinis (without which he would not fish) in a hot-water bottle since he is a notoriously poor wader and we feared either breakage or loss from a fall. This has proved extremely successful since most of his companions now think he is slightly arthritic and don't let him cut camp wood, cook, or dig the latrine. Moreover, he can carry it into his sleeping bag without arousing undue comment.

Gene Hill

Murphy

Anybody who has trundled around this blue green orb of ours long enough has become acquainted with a chap by the name of Murphy. Murphy, you see, is the author of all kinds of laws that mostly have to do with problems. It should be understood here that Murphy is not really a person, but a state of mind—a spirit, so to speak. I submit to you, gentle reader, that Murphy is the spirit of the outdoors.

Murphy's primary law says that if anything can go wrong, it will. How many times has Murphy reared his ugly head just when things looked like, for once, they were going to swing our way? Plenty. Witness.

A photographer pal, Marv Dembinsky, and I were driving by an old, overgrown, leatherleaf bog two summers ago. The day was about 95 degrees in the shade, and there wasn't any shade. As we cruised by the bog, Murphy leaned forward and whispered in Marv's ear, "That looks like a great place to photograph orchids." Dembinsky agreed and screeched to a halt. I followed—through two miles of leatherleaf that could be only navigated by lifting your knees to your chin each step. Two miles. No orchids.

Another time, John Stevens and I were duck hunting. A mallard came into our decoys far to the right, but in range. Stevens told me that if I shot, the recoil at that angle would capsize the canoe into five feet of 33 degree water. Murphy told me to shoot anyway. Stevens was right. Some places on me are still wet.

Murphy has been my constant companion on other hunting trips. Among other things, Murphy has whispered convincingly that:

That mean bull in the big pasture had finally gone to the meat market in the sky and it was safe to cross.

That I shouldn't worry about not having enough shells because the corner grocery 12,000 miles from town always carries 20-gauge shells.

Leaving the bird dog unattended in the Jeep was OK because he didn't like the taste of seat upholstery.

And, of course, I could easily vault that barbed wire fence.

Other times, Murphy's quotes have been almost prophetic. He has purred in my ear: "Sure that rock looks slippery, but you won't fall. That's where the trout are rising, just jump over there and never mind that 12 foot hole just downstream."

"OK, so a gale is blowing up on the lake, but the motor has enough gas to get you back, keep on fishing—it can't get much worse."

"No, no, don't worry, that little pool can't possibly be deeper than your waders."

"Listen, Stupid, I'm telling you that that log WILL hold you. Go ahead and cross and don't look down at the creek."

"You wouldn't possibly have come here to take wild-flower pictures in the rain, 68 miles from home, flat on your belly in a bog, and not have remembered to load the camera."

"Naw, it just looks like rain. It'll clear off by noon so just wear a light vest and jeans. You'll be fine."

"Pitch your tent right here in this little 'ole gully. The only thing that would hurt is if it rained, and it hasn't for a month."

"Go ahead and take a little mid-summer fishing trip. Calling in sick is OK because there's no way your boss will ever see you leave town at 5 a.m."

"Listen, I'm positive you've got enough money in the

checking account to buy that new gun without your wife finding out. The only way she'd know is if the check bounced."

"Go ahead and sneak off this Sunday and go fishing. You'll be back in plenty of time to take your wife to her mother's like you've been promising."

"That's a safe bet, no way is that seven-year-old, red-headed kid of yours going to outfish you this trip. Besides, what would he do with 20 bucks anyhow?"

"Trust your own sense of direction, not your 11-year-old daughter's. The road is THAT way, right through that swamp."

I can tell by the look on your face, you've met my pal Murphy a time or two. Next time you see him, don't mention me. I'm hoping he leaves me alone for a while.

Steve Smith

Dentists

My good friend, Willis Paine, sent me a package that contained a book. When I opened it, the book carried the title *All I Know About Shooting*. And beneath the title was my name as author. Inside, the pages were all blank. But Bill is a dentist and since it's common knowledge that the whirring of the high-speel drill does strange things to their brains, we have to give dentists a little liberty in what they consider to be funny.

Now, we all know that most dentists quickly attain the financial status of an Indian raja and live forever admidst splendors.

But life isn't always what it seems. The money isn't always greener in the other fellow's job. Bill, like so many dentists, is a crack field shot. But his inability to hit trap and skeet targets is really funny. (Much funnier, really, than a book filled with blank pages!) As much as I coached him, Bill absolutely failed to improve. Fortunes were dangled before gunsmiths in the vain hope that an alteration in a stock or the change of a rib could solve the mystery.

His wardrobes of cashmere and silk shooting jackets were completely retailored lest the least impedance in his mounting and swinging of the shotgun should occur. Nothing worked. Then it finally dawned on me. Everytime a dentist says "PULL"—or even hears it—he instinctively closes his eyes to avoid the anguish on his patient's face. This reflex is irreversible and accounts for the fact that to the best of my knowledge the longest run of targets of any dental surgeon has never exceeded four or five.

Gene Hill

Smelt Dipping

There is a peculiar rite of spring that will unfold about mid-April in the Great Lakes involving late hours, wet feet, and a slender little silvery fish known as the smelt.

Now the smelt is the most inoffensive of creatures, preferring to live out its days in the depths of the Great Lakes. But as warm spring rains wash their way to the lakes, these fish seek the mouths of streams, swimming up them to spawn. Therein, as they say, lies the rub.

When word goes out that the smelts are "running" (a difficult feat for a finned creature with a top speed of .4 miles per hour), all kinds of folks flock to the lakes to catch them while the catchin' is good.

I, alas, fell victim to smooth-talking smelters with a long-handled net while standing to my waist in possibly the coldest water known to man.

It went something like this: Mr. X called to sing the praises of the good, rugged, outdoor life one balmy, spring evening last April. Being an agreeable type, I allowed as how it would be nice to get out and about, having been trapped inside for one of Michigan's typical seven month winters. The trap had been sprung. Mr. X and his sidekick Mr. Y arrived at my house about 9 p.m. Waders were thrust into my hand and I was rudely shoved into their car for the drive to a secret spot known only to them and an Indian guide they had bribed and 1,200 other smelt dippers, all of whom, with their progeny for two generations, were in attendance that night. The smelts, it is said, run only at night. I think this is a ploy used by dippers to get out of the house after dark—your average smelt dipper not being trustworthy as I was finding out.

There must also be a scientific correlation between the amount of water that can seep into borrowed waders with a six inch gash in each boot and the amount of spirits you must consume to keep warm. My legendary distaste for the grape prevented me from exploring this further. It turns out that for some, smelt dipping is a good excuse to drink beer.

There are several different classifications of smelt dippers as I was to find out. First, there is the PRO. The PRO always stays warm and dry, tows a washtub behind him to hold his catch of smelt, and never slips on mossy rocks. He is the same guy who never misses pheasants during bird season, always remembers his flashlight, and puts the cap back on the toothpaste at home. Not being like him at all, I secretly hate him.

Another type is LEATHERLUNGS. This breed can make himself heard at a distance of 12 miles on a clear night, screaming with ecstacy each time he dips a smelt. He is usually surrounded by a crowd of dippers who take him seriously and assume he has the smelt lined up in single file awaiting capture. They soon learn differently and slither away into the darkness.

LEATHERLUNGS is used by the skippers of lake going freighters to warn them of shallow water. When the smelt are running, the chortles of this bird echoing across the water are more reliable than sonar.

There is a social cluster called the OLD REGULARS. This is a kind of rod and gun club in waders. There is nobody they don't know, they always have the latest information on the run, and are always helpful to newcomers.

For example, just after I had stepped into a hole and done a "hatfloater" (that's all that remains of you above the surface), one of the regulars rushed right over and said, "Watch out, there's a hole right there." The remainder of the crowd consists of what are called ROOKIES, this reporter falling, literally, into that category. We are the ones that reflect on our sinful ways as our lives flash before our eyes an average of once very 15 minutes.

In the end, I had dipped four anemic-looking smelt, six metric tons of gravel from the stream bottom, and had flirted with a bilateral hernia while crawling up a wet stream bank with my waders full of water.

The seven of us, Mr. X, Mr. Y, myself, and my four smelt arrived back home at 4:30 a.m. on a workday morning. My comrades—excluding the smelt—carried on a litany all the way home about this being "the Life". I sat in the back seat and sulked. I swore I would never go again, but spring is coming on and it has been a long winter, so if you see a half-drowned water rat huddled in a ball on a stream bank near Au Gres in mid April along about 3 a.m., stop and say hello and check for a pulse—it'll be me impersonating a smelt dipper.

Steve Smith

A Boy's First
Fishing Trip

The western skies had lost their last bit of glow as I nudged the Jeep onto the highway that would take us home. The trailered boat hummed along behind us as the black and white stripes on the road started their monotonous flashing.

Turning to my seven-year-old son, Chris, I noticed that his eyes were still aglow from the experience of this, his first ever, real fishing trip with dear old dad.

There had been earlier fishing trips. Standing on the shore drowning worms and hooking three-inch bluegills and sunfish. On those days, I'd walked behind Chris and my other two children—Amy, 11; and Jason, 5—supervising activities, rebaiting hooks, untangling lines, and trying to dodge minute fish ripped out of the water and flung up on the bank with the speed usually associated with incoming artillery shells.

But those days were behind us now. Chris had developed into a full-blown fisherman. He could get up early, stay out late, and never have to use the shoreline, having developed the jumbo bladder necessary for fishing enjoyment.

Naturally, I decided to give the kid the benefit of my years of experience on the water. He was too young to realize yet the esteem that his father was accorded by other members of the fishing fraternity. I didn't feel it my place to fill in, yet, on how my prowess with a dry fly rod was legendary, and my casting technique with any sort of gear was nothing short of miraculous.

Still, there were questions that I felt the lad must have. Today had been a new and unique experience for him, and I'm sure he wanted to talk about it.

"Well, Son," I started off, "How did you enjoy yourself today? Did you have fun?"

"Boy, I sure did," he replied.

"Any questions about anything that happened today" I inquired.

"Well . . . yeah. Did you let me catch all the fish on purpose or were you trying, too?" His eyes were big, and his freckled nose twitched with anticipation. I knew that he wanted me to answer that I'd been trying and he just out-fished me. I felt nervous in remembering that there was more truth to that than I'd like to admit.

"Sure, I was trying. I was trying quite a bit as a matter of fact." This last statement was muttered toward the Jeep's dashboard rather than to the boy.

"Well, I also want to know why you fished all day with those little feather things that you had to cast with that long pole. What's that pole called, Dad?"

"A fly rod, pal. When you get older, you'll realize that only the best fishermen fish with a fly rod and flies. Those flies are tied onto a hook to fool the fish. I tie those too. Making and catching fish on your own flies is fun. It may be the hardest kind of fishing there is."

"Oh. Then why did you keep putting little pieces of my worms on the little flies? Does that make them taste better to the fish?"

I decided to change the subject.

"Did it look like it would be hard for you to learn to cast the flies like I was?" I hedged.

"Naw", the kid remarked, "I think I could do it. Boy, I'll have to be careful when I do it, though. I'll bet it really hurt when you hooked your ear with that one fly that once. 'Member, Dad?" My throbbing ear reminded me of the difficulty of casting with a sidewind.

"Ha—ah—yeah. I remember. By the way, don't tell Mommy that I said some of those words she doesn't like me to say around the house. That'll be our little secret, okay?" I countered.

"Okay."

"Anything else I could explain to you about today?"

"Uh—When you pull up the anchor to go to another spot, do you HAVE to dive in head first like you did that once?" I could feel his eyes boring into the side of my head as I watched the highway and formulated my answer.

"Well, no. Sometimes the anchor gets caught on the bottom and you have to pull hard to get it up." I said. In a hoarse whisper, I added, "Sometimes you pull too hard." I fidgeted in my wet underwear, silently wishing the day had been warmer when I did the big splash.

He was silent for several miles after this exchange, but I could tell he was thinking. Finally, he broke the silence.

"Dad, remember when you hooked that big bass and got him right up to the boat? He sure was a big one."

"Yes, son, I remember. He weighed about five pounds, I'd guess." I answered.

"Well, don't you think it would have been better if we'd tried to use the net to catch him instead of doing like you did, trying to hit him on the head with a pop bottle?" The kid was really pushing, now.

"I suppose. Looks like we both learned something today." I was gazing out the driver's side window, now, my eyes suddenly misty.

"Didn't you say that he was the biggest bass you'd ever got that close to before?" Chris asked.

"Yeah—he sure was." An obvious catch in my throat. "Anything else?"

"Well, just one more thing. What's a B-A-R? You sure were in there a long time when we went to shore for lunch."

"Uh—oh. That's a place where fishermen gather. Only adult fishermen can go in there, though. That's why you had to stay in the Jeep and wait." I was getting nervous. We were nearing the highway exit for our home.

"Well, Dad, what do you do in there?" The kid was persistent.

"Chris, B-A-R stands for Bait And Reconnaissance. You needed some more worms and I needed to know where the fish were biting, so I went into that place." I glanced at him and answered his next, as yet unasked question. "They were out of worms. That's why we went to the bait shop next door." I was glad to see our house approaching.

As we pulled into the driveway, Chris bailed out of the Jeep and legged it toward the house. My wife was standing on the front porch, talking to the neighbor woman, whose husband is a minister at a local church.

"Guess what, Mom? B-A-R stands for Bait And Reconnaissance something, Dad says. Boy, was he ever in there a long time. . .!!"

"Wait'll you hear about all the stuff Dad and I did today." Chris was obviously intent on filling in the little woman on every gory detail.

"I'm just dying to hear all about it." Sue was leveling a firm, steady gaze at me as the neighbor retreated for the relative sanctity of her own home. "How did you cut your hand?" She seemed curious, but unconcerned.

"Well, Dad was showing me how to fillet fish." Chris was answering for me.

"Oh, Steve. Haven't I told you to wait until you get home to fillet fish? You know that Dr. Toteff always keeps a few pints of AB negative on hand when he knows fishing season has started and you're at it again."

I could see this conversation was going nowhere, so I turned to unload the Jeep and put away the boat. Chris was anxious to help, and he was carrying on a litany about the day's events. Sweetwife listened intently, logging away the details in her memory banks.

"And just what did Daddy tell you about fishing besides all of this?" Sweetwife was interrupting the kid to get at the heart of the matter.

"He told me about lots of stuff, even about you . . ." Chris stopped short and looked at me with large eyes that showed he'd broken a confidence.

"Uh—he told me how to fool you so we could go fishing." The kid was ready to spill his guts and there was no place handy to hide.

"He said that when I get older and get a job I shouldn't ever tell a woman when I get a raise. Then, I should keep the extra money for hunting and fishing and stuff." A strange feeling of warmth started to emanate from under my shirt collar. I knew it was nothing compared to the feeling of warmth my wife was experiencing.

"Anything else?" Sweetwife clipped the words off between thin, hard lips.

"Yeah, Dad says that things like new rugs and drapes always wear out, but that good fishin' poles and shotguns get worth more and more all the time, so that's what money should be used for." I was now in a jam, with no way out.

"Dad says, too, that pretty soon he'll show me where he keeps all his really good guns and fishing stuff. It's his own secret spot up in the attic. He says you never go up there at all. It's gonna be our secret!" The kid was dangerously close to getting cut out of my will. I wondered how soon I'd have to use that will.

"Did Daddy say anything else, Chris?" Sweetwife had the same look on her face then as she did the day I bought and brought home a whole litter of setter pups and parked them in the utility room.

"Yeah." The kid started to chuckle. "Remember when he wanted to get the Jeep so bad, but you said there was nothing wrong with his old car? Guess what? Dad had the gas station man take off a pipe under the car so it sounded really loud, then he told you that the old car was really broken bad and we'd have to get a new one. Boy, Dad really was laughing hard when he told me that. He says you fell for it hook, line, 'n sinker. That's fishin' talk, Mom."

Chris rushed inside the house to fill in his siblings on his day. I busied myself with the gear, trying to look invisible and not succeeding.

Sweetwife turned on her heel and headed for the house. Standing in the open doorway, she glanced in my direction.

"Coming?" she inquired.

"Yeah, just as soon as I clean up this mess I made." I chuckled unconvincingly. "Seems the lid wasn't latched on this tackle box."

"Fine," she said, "When you get through there, I'll be upstairs, cleaning the attic."

My blood felt cold as I dropped the last lure into a tackle box tray and started toward the house.

Steve Smith

How to
Chew Tobacco

A lot of things in my life strike a lot of people as foolish—if not downright shameful—such as being seen in the company of known skeet shooters and dry-fly fishermen. But in the last year I have managed to achieve a new low, according to many of my social acquaintances, or more exactly, ex-social acquaintances. Oh hell, I might as well come right out with it: I chew tobacco.

I chew tobacco where nobody else chews tobacco—at fancy dinner parties, during cocktail hours, at business meetings, and on airplanes. I chew because I like it, and I expect to continue to chew where I please and when I please. In fact the only problem I have with the whole business is chewing *what* I please.

When I was a younger fellow I could walk into the general store and stand enthralled before an almost infinite selection of multicolored packages of snuff—both the kind you tucked under your lip and the kind you pinched between your thumb and forefinger or put on the back of your hand, then snuffed up your nose. There were plugs of chewing tobacco, small, bricklike, and efficient looking. Day's Work and Apple and Honey Cut are the few I remember. The regular chewing tobacco was offered in a multitude of cuts and flavors. I believe the most popular choices were Mechanic's Delight, Mail Pouch, Beechnut, and Red Man. The last three I can still find if I do a lot of hunting around.

But as a kid, I was a pipe smoker. The nickel corncob was within economic possibilities for me, and since my mother and father, of course, had forbidden me to smoke, I had them hidden all over: in the hen house and in the barn; in hollow trees along my trap line; and a couple down by the lake where we kept the rowboat. Cigarettes were expensive—about two packs for fifteen cents, although I seem to remember that I could buy them for a penny apiece. I would once in a great while spring for a pack of Twenty Grands or Sunshines, but for day in and day out I stuck with the pipe and a nickel paper of No. 1 George Washington. I still recall that the nickel papers were strong as a green brush fire, but I must have considered myself a pretty tough fellow, because I stuck with it. But when I struck it pretty good on the trap line or put in a day or so of paid work splitting wood for my grandfather, I temporarily moved up to Edgeworth or Model, which were twice as expensive.

I know I tried chewing because a lot of the men I admired chewed, but I just couldn't make a go of it. There was a romance about chewing and spitting in the coal scuttle while yarning around the stove. I wished I could have pulled it off, but I had to be content with whatever small dash I could exhibit by lighting kitchen matches under my thumbnail or on the bottom of my front teeth and by firing up my pipe without showing that I had burned my thumb and that the inside of my mouth tasted of sulphur. All the while I kept an eye peeled for my mother or father or my kid brother, who was forever squealing on me at home about smoking.

You know how things like that stick with you. And the picture of an old bird shooter pausing for emphasis while he dipped into his pack of Red Man and filled his cheek, and worked it down to the spot where it felt just right, has over the years taken on an aura that could not be denied.

About a year ago I began sneaking a little Copenhagen snuff when I was out in the field or out fishing or up on the tractor. I liked it all right. I still will dip a little when the mood comes on me, but that still wasn't chewing. Things came to some sort of head when my wife found out that my daughter, who was then attending kindergarten, was sneaking a little snuff in her lunch box. I knew she took a little grain or two when she was with me on the tractor, and I thought it was cute and let it go at that, but my household is not a democracy—I wasn't allowed to vote. Neither was Jennifer.

Anyway, there comes a time in a man's life when he's got to have the courage to stand up to his wife and daughters, however awesome that confrontation can become, and however mightily he would wish it were otherwise, so I got hold of some Pay Car and started in. Now it's one thing to want to chew, and it's another thing to do it. You have to learn how—and I went at it solo. You learn first off that chewing is a misnomer. You don't *chew,* you just take an amount, which you determine by your personal physical make-up, tuck it in your face between the gum and the cheek and more or less leave it alone.

Right off, let me tell you that you don't ever need a spittoon, if you calculate the amount right. If you're in a duck blind and want to test yourself against an incoming wind, you can enjoy the skills of expectoration, but you don't absolutely have to spend your day watering the area around you.

Time passes, and the more I chewed, the more I liked it, but I knew something was amiss: there was a void in this new sport, and that was variety. It's hard enough where I live to get chewing tobacco at all, and to have the freedom of choice among flavors, cuts, and strengths that the men of my youth enjoyed was no longer possible. Or so I thought, until a friend of mine, as a joke, brought back for me, from a trip down South, a package filled with exotic stuff: several plugs like Bloodhound, Brown Mule, Black Maria, and Bull of the Woods; and a few papers of chewing tobacco called Red Fox. The package itself was a work of art, and as I tucked away a modest amount, I felt delight that must have been near to what Pierre Perignon felt when he first tasted champagne. You've heard that every man deserves to have one good gun and one good dog. I add to that one perfect chewing tobacco.

It didn't take too long until I'd gone through what he'd

brought me, and it took less time to discover that no one, absolutely no one, for what appeared to be a hundred miles around, sold it. It seemed that I had but just discovered the ne plus ultra of chews only to realize that I might as well have only dreamed it.

I happened to wistfully mention my lost love to a close neighbor, Tom Young, whom I knew hailed from South Carolina, and whom I knew for a fact was returning there to visit his family. Before too long, Tom had promised to strip the state of Red Fox and that after his return I would never want again. Tom left on his trip, and after a week or so I began to scan his driveway, hoping to see his car. Then I'd think that maybe he'd forgotten anyway, and I'd console myself with something else.

I'd about given up on Tom when late one night, he knocked on my door and handed me a paper bag with a note on it. He left saying he'd just that minute gotten home and had to go back and help his wife get the luggage out of his car. I shook open the bag and a dozen packages of Red Fox fell on the kitchen table. I couldn't get a handful quick enough! When I was contentedly rolling an ounce or so from one jaw to the other, I picked up Tom's note and read it: "My grandfather, who has been in the business, told me that the secret of good tobacco was not altogether in the leaf. He said that one had to take a mind to how it's cured. Some folk stroke up their fires too fast and they burn it right up. And others are so afraid of burning it that they let their barn get too cold, and it cures green. Good tobacco has to be properly dried, then cured, and finally fixed at successively higher temperatures.

"Nowadays, when one is forced to cross the country in a few hours and drink three-day-old beer, ain't it a pleasure to know, as I'm sure you do, that good friends, good bourbon, and good tobacco are slowly made."

Gene Hill

Hunting Pal's Shortcomings

Despite the pleadings of their wives, a rather large assortment of fellas tend to troop through my house during the shooting season. These guys are, for the most part, upstanding individuals who, save this one fault, do their part for the economy, society, and so forth. I've taken to noticing, however, that lately whenever one of these guys falls on by the house, one corner of what passes for my office is occupied by a small, freckle-faced kid who lives with me—my older son, Chris.

Now Chris—who also answers to "Boom" (although I think he secretly hates that name but that's what I call him so he doesn't say anything)—delights in sitting around listening to the stories, most of which are lies, about the hunting or fishing, or whatever the guys have been involved in.

Lately, I've been taking him along when I figure that the going won't be too tough, when there aren't too many other people around, or when his begging and kissing of my hunting boots finally makes me give in. I've noticed that when he DOES go along, he does have a few shortcomings.

For example, the kid never, but never, chips in for his share of the gas, always bellies up to the counter of a backwoods grocery store with his hands full of the type of stuff his mother doesn't let him eat at home (and which I spring for when Sweetwife isn't around), and constantly badgers me about how old you have to be to go hunting and carry a gun.

He does, however, have some redeeming qualities which allow him to go as often as he does. He's always interested in seeing any new plant or fall wildflower he hasn't seen before (I made him memorize *Sprianthes cernua*, the name of a pretty little fall orchid I ran across while grouse hunting this past autumn. He was quite impressed with himself that he knew the name of this little Nodding Ladies' Tresses orchid, and remembers the Latin even if he IS a little shaky on the common name).

Boom's also very willing to take care of the things that need to be done on any hunting trip. He takes care of the bird-dog petting quite nicely.

Boom also handles all the fetching of equipment prior to the hunt, and is an expert at boot-pulling-off after we're home.

For my part, I repay his actions by making sure the branches don't snap back in his face, pointing out some type of tree or shrub, buying treats, showing him chipmunk holes and bird nests, and explaining why the dog stiffens up and points when a bird is near.

But, with so few things a man can leave his kids these days, what I really try to do is give him an appreciation for the outdoors and hope it will be as large a part of his life as it has been mine.

I don't think he could ever ask for more.

Steve Smith

It's No Snap Raising a Young Photographer

I'd like this to serve as a warning to all parents that they'd better watch who their kids are hanging out with. My daughter, Amy, is into all the stuff that young, teenage females are into. She's a cheerleader, likes slumber parties (where they apparently never slumber, but do everything else), and thinks one kid on the junior high basketball team is kind of nice. However, that's not the problem.

For years, she's been quite interested and quite good at identifying plants. She can rattle off the Latin and common names of most of the trees in this area (although the oaks give her a rough time in that her *Quercus albas* and *Quercus macrocarpas* get turned around lately).

But, back to the original story. Marv Dembinsky is a good friend of mine and a noted and talented outdoor photographer. Marv has all kinds of photos of wild plants and outdoor scenes that are so good that I hate him for his skill. I take the odd picture now and again, but I prefer to spend my cash on shotguns rather than lenses.

Marv has, however, found a clean slate with Amy. He has got her so interested in outdoor photography that she baked me for a 35mm camera not long ago and started taking pictures. I was surprised when I found the quality of her shots. They are great! Nothing like a set of 14-year-old eyes to get things in perfect focus, and Marv's coaching on our trips afield in the spring have done wonders for her composition.

The problem is, Marv is making noises to her, and she's repeating them distrubingly often, about a camera called a "Nikon," which can be had for an amount slightly less than the national debt of Peru. Last summer, on one of our trips to the woods, Marv was explaining to her how such cameras have great lenses of every conceivable style and magnification, and about how she should pester me about one.

I, for my part, stayed behind and turned cold inside. I mean, for the price of a Nikon, I could buy a pretty decent Winchester Model 23 in 20 gauge. Also, since Amy isn't presently employed, I get to pay for film and developing!

Well, what do I do?

You're right, but maybe I can hold her off until she's 15 anyway.

Steve Smith

The
Happy Wife

In the old days, the wife of a hunter was kept involved with his fortunes a good deal more than is true today. When a man went forth with his matched pair of spears (probably the equivalent of improved cylinder for short throws and full choke for the longer) and returned in his own good time, his wife got down to the chores of skinning, cutting up the meat, and discussing with him the advantages of twenty-four-lines-per-inch checkering on the spear shaft as opposed to eighteen or twenty. She was interested in how he felt about the balance of his clubs, axes, and the like, and clung to his every word as she patiently chewed the skins to the suppleness of his liking.

The nostalgic beauty of such a tranquil scene is, of course, almost irrevocably lost to us. You arrive home tired, thirsty, and eager to tell the Queen Bee what a helluva fellow she was lucky enough to garner when you're reminded that she has spent all day waxing and polishing the floor. If you make a feeble joke about "at least the mop handle has a nice piece of wood even it if seems to be a trifle butt-heavy," you may be accused of having spent most of the day at Mario's Cherry Croft Inn.

I think she tends to stay apart from the long, detailed conversations about choke boring and the perilous indecision you might someday have to conquer in the selection of side locks over box locks because she lacks the involvement of her ancestors. Simply, we have been too selfish.

I have made a point (never mind the obvious self-sacrifice) of not only permitting but encouraging my wife to pick and clean every bird I bring home. Never mind that the local poultry shop in Easton, Maryland, will do the complete job on my Canada geese for a dollar or so— bring mine home en plumage. I'm sure that part of the deep pleasure my wife exhibits in serving rabbit stew is the fact that I bought her a nice light skinning knife for her last birthday and taught her how to use it.

Right now I'm part way finished on a project that will bring tears to her eyes: a custom-made linoleum kitchen flooring designed to resemble exactly the muddy footprints of English setters, Labrador retrievers, and the sole prints of my Gokey and Bass boots and my insulated waders—so real that you'd believe we'd all just stepped out of the swamp.

This, when completed, should obviate the necessity of mopping and waxing the floor forever and release her so she can spend more time reloading my trap shells for me, keeping my field clothes mended, and boning up my boots with Sno-Pruf. In the winter evenings before the fire she takes great delight in carefully cleaning the checkering on my shotguns and palming warm linseed oil into the stocks while I read her tidbits from Thomas's *Shotgun Lore for the Sportsman,* or advice from Churchill on wing shooting. For a special treat, I recall exactly for her every decent score I've ever made on trap or skeet, with special emphasis on the misfortunes beyond my control that caused the occasional miss.

Rest assured that I am doing everything in my power to convince the management of outdoor magazines to include a woman's editor, creating a special section for our wives. There'll be patterns so they can make our hunting clothes for us, exercises to strengthen their wrists so they can work a hand trap to help us sharpen our shooting eye, and the like.

An example of what ingenuity women can achieve when they're on the right track is the discovery my wife made when she was testing the performance of some $7\frac{1}{2}$s she had loaded for my trap gun. From 40 yards they'll penetrate to page 203 of Kate Millet's book, *Sexual Politics.*

Gene Hill

The Answer Man
Shoots Golfs

Dear Answer Man,
I have been invited by my boss to go "golf shooting" with him and some important clients. Not wishing to appear ignorant, I'd like a little information about this sport before I go. Frankly, I haven't heard of golfs at all and I'm in the dark. Please fill me in.
Chester

Dear Chester,
Aha! Golfs! I have a little experience with these creatures, and feel happy that you came to the Source for your help.

My experience with shooting golfs happened several years ago when two gentlemen (I'll call them Joe and Frank) asked me if I would like to try this version of organized lunacy. Not having the Source to guide me (as you are so fortunate to have, all false modesty aside), I agreed with some trepidation.

These two picked me up and we headed for the golfs shooting grounds. Now, right off, I was turned off. They brought no dogs and walk-up shooting without dogs ranks, for me, right next to a root canal on the pleasure scale. In any event, I agreed that perhaps there was something here to learn.

Arriving at the shooting grounds, I found that Frank and Joe harbored sadistic streaks heretofore cleverly concealed—they were going to do their hunting with what they called "golf clubs." Naturally, I had visions of the Canadian harp seal hunt, squabbles with Greenpeace, and maybe your odd restraining order from a bleeding-heart-commie-pinko federal judge. But, I perservered.

I noticed rather quickly that golfs had an overpopulation problem. They had evidently grazed the grass down to where it wouldn't have kept together the body and soul of an undersized goat. There appeared to be no winter-over cover, just a few trees here and there with virtually no understory of shrubs to foil any avian predators.

I also noticed that there seemed to be a large number of other hunters, dressed in loud colors to avoid being clubbed, I assumed. The sweaters they wore all had little alligators on the breast, and I took this as some sort of initiation badge denoting bravery.

We checked in at the clubhouse and paid our shooting fee. Frank looked at me funny when I asked how many golfs were released for our party for the 10 bucks I just plunked down.

Moving out onto the shooting grounds, I watched as my two cohorts changed into spiked shoes, which naturally made me nervous. I mean, I hate hunting game that has to be stomped on to finally reduce to possession. I was given some of the clubs, and when I asked about their use, Joe told me something about distance, which I translated into meaning that the club with a "9" on it was like improved cylinder and the big club (an antique—still made of wood) with the "1" on it was like full choke. After that, I got a little fuzzy.

It soon became apparent that you searched for golfs by looking in their holes. Evidently, the creatures stay in colonies of exactly 18 such habitats, and hunting them consists of walking from spot to spot and looking in the holes. I wondered how we could have any luck doing this because it seemed to me that the hunters just before us were doing the same thing and having no luck.

And here, I must add an amusing footnote: golf hunting is so unproductive, that the hunters amuse themselves by knocking a little white ball around (which I first mistook for a golf egg) from hole to hole. This apparently is the golf hunter's equivalent of the gin rummy game that keeps goose hunters occupied between flights. I figured as long as you have to walk from hole to hole, that hitting the little ball with the club was as good a way as any to keep my sanity.

In fact, I once hit my little ball toward the next golf hole (marked with a *flag*—can you believe it, talk about a tame preserve) and the darn thing went into the golf hole on the first hit. Frank and Joe looked shocked, and I was mad—I had to walk all the way to the hole with nothing to do except watch those two jerks!

Anyhow, Frank kept writing on a little card, evidently a way that he cooperates with the game department about how many golfs we sighted (or didn't). But, the sonuvagun lied. He said that, at the end, he had seen 84 golfs, Joe had seen 90, and I had seen 141 golfs! Whattacrock! I never saw one! And, since he claimed I had the highest total, *I* had to buy the mash 'n splash!

So, golf hunters have to be put in the same category as trap shooters, snipe hunters, and other similar, emotionally unstable folks—not to be trusted.

So, Chester, I wish you luck. If you shoot any golfs, send me a picture of one, fercryinoutloud.
AM

Steve Smith

A Million Dollars

There's a rather well-known short story about two office girls who played a game at lunch called "What would you do if you had a million dollars?" One day they started their game just as they were passing the window of a famous New York jewelry store, and one of them noticed a magnificent diamond necklace in the window. "I'd start off buying that," she said. But they began to argue about how much such a necklace could be until they finally went in and asked. The salesman smiled at such an unlikely pair shopping for diamonds but graciously showed them the price tag: $1,200,000.

I'll admit that thinking about what I'd do if I were rich takes up more of my time than it should; time that should be spent replacing shingles on my leaking roof or digging a drainage ditch in my flooded field—chores that I'm well aware do not eat up too much of those more well-to-do.

But do you realize how much the cost of being rich has gone up? It's getting so bad that a reasonable man today can hardly afford to daydream without getting embarrassed.

I felt pretty comfortable dreaming about owning a side-by-side Purdey or Holland when they only cost $2,500, but now that the base price has moved up to about $15,000 with a three-to-four-year wait, I simply can't afford it.

A friend just sold a beautiful Leonard fly rod for $500, and all the while I'd been dreaming of owning one at the imaginary price of about $150. I suddenly felt like Rip Van Winkle!

You've been dreaming of fishing for Atlantic salmon in Norway for about $1,500 a week? Try doubling that, you're still dreaming at the old prices. How about a safari in Africa with a first class hunter for $200 a day? You might as well ask the orchestra to play you a lindy hop or try to find a nice comfortable pair of high-button dress shoes to wear.

The pipes I used to like, and saved for, because they were good buys even at the incredible price of $12 now start at around $50. My old nickel paper of tobacco costs 85¢.

About the only thing we can keep down to a reasonable level is our income—that doesn't seem to have gotten involved with inflation.

So I've had to lay back a bit on dreaming and put more effort into handling the day-to-day. I always made a small thing about being fairly well dressed for bird hunting. That is, being neat and clean, not wearing overalls and galoshes. But my favorite hunting pants that I used to go through at the rate of two pair a season, at about $15 a pair, now start at twice that. Which means I've got to pay a lot more attention to the width of the strands in barbed wire fences and be a bit more strict with my dogs on retrieving in briars.

I'm perfectly willing, as usual, to let my thoughts wander to what might have been, but considerably scaled down; reality is about as far as the mind can travel today without being overly taxed—in more ways than one.

Money being out of the question—the opportunity's now denied us, we come to the hoarding of time, and find, sadly, that time as well has sifted through our fingers like the sands of a broken hourglass. Yet to dream a bit about it is possible, but as with money, still tinged by sadness.

We have all looked ahead to owning time that could be spent in lieu of other commodities. Time to boil a few pine knots to mold into decoy heads. Time to fine-hone a pointing dog. Time to checker a stock, work a knife from a file and ax out a paddle. Time to learn to tie flies. Time to craft a rod or make a boat. And time to learn to use them well. Time to see where the river sprang from a spring, time to see past the horizon, time to listen to the birds and smell the pines, time to see where the bear went over the mountain and see what he could see.

Remember when time was cheap? The songs we sang about it told us that we had time on our hands, that time stood still, that tomorrow would be time enough. And now we find it was not so.

Suddenly times to come have become times past, and we must hoard it and spend it as cautiously as the tag ends of a small inheritance, which is what it really was all along— except no one told us.

So we find now that the skills we dreamed of are scant and awkward. The time came to choose between spending money or time, and most of us chose money—because as little as we had of it, we had more of it than time.

Our decoys, one or two or so, are pathetic, awkward birds that never came alive from wood. A dog or so was worked just enough to be called "passable" by closer friends, but the knives I use are not shaped by my hand, and my paddles have none of the warm idiosyncrasies of my carving.

I bum flies and borrow the rods I dreamed of making. The mountain that I waited so long to cross is woven with tar roads, and the bear is a remnant from stories of others and trips to the zoo with children.

But regret cannot be bundled up like a foundling and left late at night on another's doorstep, to be someone else's responsibility. And although I did few of the things I once dreamed of—I've done a good many things that please me much.

Having made my bed, so to speak, I find myself lying in it with less discomfort than I might. Should I someday, like an ancient king, command that all my goodies be brought before me that I might survey from my counterpane what I made of my life's pleasures the panorama would not be too displeasing.

Instead of my own masterful decoys I have a handful of the real masters: Ira Jester, Captain Joseph Lincoln, and Ira

Hudson. A couple of knives by the likes of Loveless and Russell. A shotgun or two and a fly rod or so that I'm not ashamed to be seen with in public. I could extend the list a bit, but fearful of family reprisals and trades by my more astute friends, I forebear.

A friend of mine who was an avid and far above average golfer once overhead his boss telling someone, "You show me a man who plays to a four handicap, and I'll show you a man who doesn't give too much thought to his job."

You show me a man who has a house badly in need of paint, a closetful of shotguns and rifles, walls covered with prints of bird dogs and sporting scenes but no furniture and an untrimmed lawn filled with retrievers, and I'll show you a man who spent his life dreaming, with very few regrets.

The money I've earned I've spent like a sailor on leave, and the time I promised to put in on useful endeavors I've spent skylarking with similar minded friends; exchanging daydream for daydream about what magnificent things we would have if we were rich—and the wonderful things we would accomplish if only we ever had the time.

Gene Hill

Listen Up

Well, gang here it is—(sound of drum roll in the background) the First Annual Outdoor Quiz (trumpet flourish). You can enter as many times as you wish—or can stomach. Got your pencil? Good.

1. When you are grouse hunting and your dog refuses to come when called, you should:

_____ Curse openly and elaborately.

_____ Cry.

_____ Tell your partner that you were afraid this would happen because the vet had warned you the dog was about to go deaf.

2. You awaken to a howling gale with rain and sleet in early November on a Saturday. You should:

_____ Go back to bed.

_____ Go duck hunting.

_____ Go duck hunting and sleep in the blind.

3. On a trout fishing trip, your pal is catching nice fish from a pool downstream from you. You should:

_____ Muddy up the water for him.

_____ Chuck rocks into the pool to ask if that's about where they're hitting.

_____ Float a bottle with an obscene note in it down to him.

4. While checking out a good-looking woodcock cover in the middle of a pasture, you are attacked by a Hereford

bull. The bull chases your pal as you gain safety beyond the fence. You should now:

_____ Distract the bull from your pal.

_____ Offer advice to your buddy.

_____ Offer advice to the bull.

5. On a pheasant hunting trip, your dog finds and eats the first bird your partner shoots. You should:

_____ Curse the dog and apologize to your friend.

_____ Look the other way and feign ignorance.

_____ Act relieved and tell your pal that you are glad the mutt's appetite has improved because he's hardly been eating at all.

6. A friend you took to a good hunting spot goes back with HIS buddy at a later time. You find out about it. You should:

_____ Let the air out of his tires.

_____ Have your wife call his and ask for him in a sensuous voice and refuse to leave her name.

_____ Cross him off your Christmas card list.

_____ Tell his boss where he REALLY was that week in October.

_____ All of the above.

7. Your kid's teacher won't let him take a week from school to go fishing. You should:

_____ Invite the teacher.

_____ Tell the teacher it's a living geography lesson.

_____ Mail the teacher a fish—from New Brunswick.

8. Your wife announces that your favorite niece is getting married on the opening Saturday of trout season and she wants you to give her away. You should:

_____ Claim not to know the child.

_____ Ask if waders and fishing vest can be dyed black.

_____ Weep piteously for a minimum of 10 days.

9. Your pal has just scored his first ever double on grouse. You should:

_____ Praise his skill and marksmanship.

_____ Pretend to have something in your eye that stopped you from seeing it.

_____ Pretend to reload your own gun while asking him if he shot too.

Fun so far? You bet! Now we will move into a different phase of the quiz. This is the outdoor knowledge section of the test.

10. A compass always points:

_____ North.

_____ Toward your house.

_____ Toward your gun barrel because you held it too close—again.

11. The biggest mistake made by beginning bow hunters is:

_____ Losing their little sticks.

_____ Trying to shoot through trees.

_____ Beginning bow hunting in the first place.

12. The gun you really need is:

_____ Too expensive.

_____ Not available.

_____ Owned by your Uncle Abbot and his favorite nephew is a flower arranger named Julius.

13. Your dog gets car sick in the back of your buddy's new car. The best response to this situation is to:

_____ Open the window.

_____ Admire the absorbancy of today's new fabrics.

_____ Both of the above.

14. Every sportsman knows that a spikehorn has how many points?

_____ One.

_____ Two.

_____ Buckle my shoe.

15. With all the monthly payments at home due at once, a good bass boat comes up for sale. What is the best course of action?

_____ Make sure the boat is seaworthy.

_____ See if the boat needs a point job or if she's ready to go right now.

_____ Ask if the motor is included.

16. You discover a grouse cover actually teeming with the birds. The best thing to do is:

_____ Invite Steve Smith.

_____ Invite Steve Smith and Gene Hill.

_____ Invite the authors of this book.

17. Ducks seem to fly and decoy the best under which of these conditions?

_____ When you're out of shells.

_____ Just as the boat starts to leak.

_____ Two minutes after legal shooting time has ended.

18. Which of these gifts makes the best, belated, anniversary present to your wife?

_____ A Diana grade Browning skeet gun

_____ An Art Neumann fly rod

_____ A shot-shell reloader

19. One of the best ways to be sure you're ready for deer hunting is to:

_____ Run around the block each night, pulling the neighbor kids on a slab of concrete.

_____ Run up the municipal parking ramp while carrying a refrigerator.

_____ Memorize the following: three of a kind beats two pair, a flush beats a straight, a full house beats a flush, and the last card in seven-card stud is dealt face down, regardless of local rules.

20. While waterfowling in gale winds, your partner starts blowing his brand new duck call, giving all indications he is trying to attract mortally wounded wildebeast (I'm sure this problem is nothing gnu to you) and is, as a result, scaring hell out of not only any ducks within earshot but also the Ladies' Aid Society which is meeting $3\frac{1}{2}$ miles downwind. Your response should be:

_____ Ask to see his call and then throw it as far out into the decoys as possible, using an overhand motion.

_____ Ask to see his call and then throw it as far as possible AWAY from the decoys, using an overhand motion.

_____ Place partner's duck call around his neck and throw entire entourage into the decoys.

21. While asking permission to hunt from a farmer, the two of you are distracted by the sounds of your pointer pulling the farmer's wife's clean laundry from the clothesline.

You should:

_____ Comment that the dog must like the farmer because he doesn't rip up just ANYBODY'S sheets.

_____ Offer to purchase the laundry.

_____ Admire the cleanliness of the laundry and offer to purchase the farmer's wife.

22. Your new Lab will go on his first ever hunting trip with you and your partner. All summer you have bored partner stiff with tales of the dog's retrieving prowess. On the first hunt, with partner watching critically, the dog will retrieve all of these EXCEPT:

_____ A dead carp.

_____ Your partner's thermos.

_____ The decoys.

_____ Ducks.

23. While ordering a custom-built, English "best" gun, you offhandedly (and, I might add tactlessly) inquire about the cost. Upon hearing the sum you:

_____ Stagger backward, watching the room swirl around through tear-shrouded vision.

_____ Immediately try to add up your total worldly net worth and then compute the amount of the loan you'll need to supplement this figure.

_____ Consider the help of your wife and children in light of the white slavery market.

_____ Comment that the sum compares favorably with the Gross National Product of Bolivia.

24. While putting out decoys in deep water with you watching from the boat, your partner suddenly goes under in 33 degree water with pounding waves. You should:

_____ Take his picture if/when he surfaces.

_____ At the top of your lungs, ask him if you can have his decoys and boat in the event he doesn't bounce back from this one.

_____ Ask him if it's REALLY true that waders full of water act like an anchor.

25. While pheasant hunting near a cow pasture, you try to step over an electric fence, but instead come down and

straddle it. It is, of course, fully operational. You should:

_____ Curse all cattle in general, and these cattle in particular for requiring such devices.

_____ Curse Benjamin Franklin.

_____ Consider the monastic life.

26. The most important thing to learn concerning downhill skiing is:

_____ Don't look down from the chair lift.

_____ In the long run, it would be cheaper to buy a set of condominiums than to take up skiing.

_____ Thou shalt not get thy cast wet.

27. To test the strength of the ice before venturing out to ice fish, the proper procedure is to:

_____ Take along someone who weighs more than you to walk ahead of you.

_____ There is no second choice.

28. One of the best ways to keep the old garage full of firewood all winter is to:

_____ Steal it from your neighbors.

_____ Follow the tree trimming trucks around and beg scraps they leave behind.

_____ Chop up your furniture.

29. When riding a snowmobile, the first rule you should always observe is:

_____ Snowmobiles do not have roll bars.

_____ Snowmobiles can't swim and indeed don't even float very well.

_____ Exposed skin at 50 mph freezes before you can say "whereinheckaremydoggonemittens?"

30. You can tell when you're about to freeze when:

_____ The film in your camera breaks when you advance it.

_____ Your fingers break when you advance the film.

_____ You wonder if you HAVE spent too much time hunting and fishing, like your wife claims.

There you go, good luck.

Steve Smith

Playing Dog

Among the more embarrassing aspects of my life, as I reflect back on it, is the fact that for a period of time, I—uh—hunted grouse and woodcock without a dog.

I know, that borders on heresy if not sacrilege, and I don't do it anymore, honest. Even at the time, I knew I must be violating some form of oath sworn by all grouse and woodcock hunters with a hand on W. H. Foster's *New England Grouse Shooting*. But, I had no dog, no coin of the realm with which to buy a dog, and no buddies with dogs. Sort of stuck.

What I did have, however, were a few pals with what could be described as, "speed-limit IQ's," what Joel Vance calls, "apprentice morons." With these guys, I saved a ton of dough on dog food.

In my early days of hunting, I quickly learned that grouse and woodcock lived way down deep in the thick stuff. I learned that if I went down in there after them, I got cut and scratched. I also learned I didn't *like* going down there to get them and I learned I hurt a lot less if I got the *other* guy to go down there after them.

So, the problem became getting a hunting buddy that was willing to go down there, rouse the birds into the air, and I could stand back, take the open shots, and carry on a litany about "being here."

I could see it all: unsoiled clothing, unscathed shanks,

delightful autumn days—all thanks to a pal who would play dog.

In order that you not think me conniving, let me point out that the position of *Homo canine* was not without glamour. The guy would lead the league in tree-limb shooting, cornea scratching, and artery opening. In short, he'd get his share of the action, albeit of a different sort.

As things turned out, getting the other guy to play dog made me into a man. Here's how.

The first guy I ever recruited was Alan Fernbeak, Southside High School classmate, star football player, and chip-on-the-shoulder-resident Neanderthal. He was big, burly, tough as a twenty-penny nail, and had an IQ on a good day that hovered right around the freezing point. "Mr. Fernbeak," as those of us possessed of our faculties called him to his face, made it through high school with the aid of those of us who coached him on the intricasies of the academic life—like opening his locker and counting out his 35¢ for lunch.

All through the early days of autumn, Al and I plotted out forays against the grouse and woodcock. Al agreed (so, naturally, I agreed) that we would be "out there" popping brush and hurling limbs away from our bodies like diving linebackers.

Came Opening Day.

I pick up Al in my '53 Chevy and we load his gun and gear into the car. Al is salivating. I hadn't seen Al salivate since he turned Art ("Crazy Artie") Nitzenbaum into a gym class statistic because Artie wouldn't hold the door open for him (hence the name "Crazy Artie"). I remember looking at Artie after their brief scuffle and thinking, "Gee, Artie looks like he's just sleeping."

Anyway, on Opening Day, Al wore a football jersey, tennis shoes, blue jeans, and an undersized hat (on Al, everything looked undersized). Perfect, I thought, for popping brush. Perfect, I also thought, for running down and beating to a bloody foam his hunting partner. I let the thought pass.

We arrived at the first covert of the day (in those days,

we called coverts, "places we're gonna hunt"), and Al took the car off and got his gun ready. I thought that perhaps it was unwise to let this person carry a loaded weapon, but since I didn't know any sane method of separating Al from his firepower, I let that slide by too.

"Well," says I to Al, "do you want to hunt that patch of thick stuff Al. . . ."

"What did you sayyyyyyyyyy?" he bellowed.

"allll the way over to that hill?" I finished up. Though slow of foot, I was a 4.2 man for the Quick-Thinking 40.

"Yeah," he snapped, "let's go."

"You bet, Mr. Fernbeak," I agreed. "You go down in there where the birds are and I'll stay on the outside and tell you where they fall when you shoot them, okay? Sir?"

Well, evidently it sounded good to Al because he sort of trundled off in the direction of the brush—mostly briars and blackberry canes with some thorn apples thrown in, all first-rate epidermis collectors. I slipped around toward the edge of the cover as Al entered the brush.

The sounds emanating from the bushes reminded me of the time I visited my Uncle Elrod at the meat-packing plant in Kenosha. Al swore, squealed, and yelled, and (I assumed) bled his way through the cover as I sauntered around the outside. Before too long, a woodcock hopped straight up.

BANG! I shoot. A full three seconds later, Al shoots. The bird had dropped at my shot, but Al let out a whoop. "Got 'im!!" he exclaimed. I didn't argue. I didn't make it to 17 years old being stupid.

Ten minutes more of vegetative agony, and Al moves another woodcock. I shoot the bird again, and Al wonders what I'm shooting at. I tell him nothing, that I wanted to see if my gun worked. He grunts and pushes through the cover again.

The scene was repeated four more times: Al would unknowingly flush a bird, I would shoot it and run in unnoticed to retrieve it. I kept saying I was shooting at rabbits or starlings or something. Al's voice, each time he hollered at me, was growing weaker from, I deduced, loss of blood.

Finally emerging from the cover, Al looked like who-came-in-second at the bullfight. What remained of his jeans and jersey were stained red (I prayed it wasn't blackberry juice), and one of his sneakers was missing. He still held his gun, but the stock would never, ever, be the same. Al wore a sort of bewildered, dazed, weakened look on his face. I walked over to him, took his gun from his numb fingers, and turned him toward the car.

"Yessir, you sure did a good job in there. Too bad we didn't move more birds, but you sure did a good job."

"Where are we going?" he mumbled.

"Why, to the car. Are you alright?" I asked.

"Yeah—yeah—okay—don't walk so fast, willya?"

Naturally, I walked faster and soon got ahead of Al. Reaching the car ahead of him with my five woodcock, I turned to watch him try to fight his way up a slight slope to the vehicle. He was still 100 yards away.

Then it hit me. My male adolescent need to be indominable—to be free!

"Hurry up, you fathead!" I screamed. "Even *you* can figure out we gotta go, you dumbbell." Honest, I don't know why I did it. I was crazy.

Al stopped and stood there, weaving from side to side. "Whaaaat?" he moaned. "Wait'll I git up there!"

"So what," I hollered, "What're ya gonna do, you stupid jerk." All my frustrations were coming out to the school bully. I was fighting back!

Al started up the hill, but fell, rose, and fell again. I threw his gun on the ground, got in the Chevy, and started her up.

Heading out onto the gravel road, I saw Al rise again in the rear view mirror and chuckled to myself as he pitched forward again. I thought how delighted Artie would be to hear of what I'd done to Al. I promised myself I'd stop by the Home to see Artie and tell him. On warm fall days, the nurses let Artie out onto the patio in his wheelchair.

The transfer to Franklin High across town wasn't nearly as bad as I thought it was going to be.

Steve Smith

Evasions, Excuses, and Lies

I don't expect a standing round of applause from anyone but my immediate family, but this is the first year in longer than I care to recall that I haven't gotten my hands on a new gun for the fall season. Not that I haven't been tempted, but I have managed to resist through a combination of character, self-denial, and being more or less broke.

A friend of mine who lives in Boston has a completely different outlook on things. Where I go for logic in picking up something new he cunningly goes for sentimental romance. For example; he acquired a new Labrador retriever this past January and immediately acquired a new duck gun to go with it. Having done that he now refers to the gun as "Blackie's side-by-side," thus simultaneously convincing himself of his own unselfish good-heartedness and shunting off the wrath of his wife. He recently became a father and, as he left the bar where we had toasted the joyful event, he asked my recommendation of what would make a suitable single-barrel trap gun for an eight-pound, six-ounce, baby girl.

But the thrill of buying a new gun is always there whether it's for an eight-week-old puppy or Baby Susan—and they won't outgrow it as quickly as they do a plastic bone or a pink rattle.

Of all the reasons to get your hands on a new gun, the worst one to talk about at home is necessity, unadorned. As specious as it sounds, you're better off to mumble something like "The Doc wants me to get out more often this fall but he says I need something a little lighter to carry around. He says I ought to have a little 20 gauge—add five years to my heart." Here you've taken two birds with one story: more outings, new gun. That's hard to top, but it can be done. For example, you can add one more thing—but be careful not to lose it all by being too greedy: "Doc says he doesn't want me hunting alone too much, but Vern and Jim are spending the first few days in Alabama at his uncle's quail place. . . ."

Eliciting a wife's sympathy to the point where she has memorized your stock measurements, or digs into the egg money so you can work over a few coveys down South is usually the result of script writing and acting worth an Academy Award. If some of the stories I've heard delivered to wives were set to music you'd leave the theater whistling the hit tune.

For sheer difficulty (say No. 9 on a scale of 1 to 10) the Mt. Everest of accomplishment is bringing home a new dog just after your wife has totally redecorated the house: draperies, slipcovers, and carpeting. To my knowledge this has only happened once, and it was accomplished by the head of a major oil company who deposited a large sum of money in escrow with his wife's attorney to pay for damages, if any. It can also be accomplished by sheer frontal assault combined with wit and great presence of mind. For example, a Mr. Richard W. purchased a puppy at a Ducks Unlimited dinner while in a state of tremendous conviviality. He arrived home shortly before dawn, climbed in bed with the puppy snuggled up against his chest and dropped into a deep sleep which was shortly interrupted by his wife. He opened one eye and saw her standing over him, pointing at the puppy's head on the pillow. "What's that?" she shouted.

He closed the eye, smiled, and said, "Congratulate me. I've just had a German shorthair pointer."

The true gamesman tests his mettle constantly and is much to be admired by those of us less dedicated—and he has much to offer us. Jim Rikhoff, who hates hunting in tough

cover, has developed an excellent variation on the old Mitchell Maneuver. (Mitchell, who was chronically unable to connect with a crossing bird, took to wearing an eyepatch and
chattering about pupillary occlusion so we would always let
him walk up behind the dog and take all the straightaways.)

Rikhoff would show up for a partridge hunt with his
face covered with a thick white salve that closely resembled
zinc oxide ointment and would talk, most embarrassed and
self-consciously, about being allergic to dried leaves. It wasn't
until he'd made six consecutive misses on birds in the open
that we discovered that the lotion was compounded of vanilla
cake frosting heavily laced with Spanish brandy. This also
explained the reason why after several shoots he had to be
driven home, due to reapplying the mixture with too heavy
a hand at too frequent intervals.

You must remember that a too-involved ruse is easily
forgotten in moments of crisis or excitement and that the
simple tried-and-true variety is still the most effective. Take
the Editor's Evasion, named for a magazine man who had
taken to wearing boots of different sizes. His left boot was
a size 8 while the right was a 13EE. Years before he had
broken his foot and had discovered while shooting skeet in
a walking cast that he was able to make a much more fluid
pivot on right-crossing birds.

Even though his foot had long since healed he continued, wisely, to bravely explain about swelling in the ankle.
He managed very nicely to avoid any hard walking and could
be found as often as possible taking right-hand birds with
incredible consistency due to the ease of swing he had managed with his foot flopping loosely in the one huge boot.
Being a penurious devil (all editors are) he'll find some excuse
in the next year or so for being able to wear the big left boot
to get full mileage out of the mismatched pairs. Lacking much
imagination, he'll be around with some story about being
bitten in the ankle by a tarpon, or some other such malarkey.

We see the true sportsman, then, as fully dedicated to
coming out on top amid his friends and family, one who will
surely find means to create golden assets out of his leaden

liabilities. His shortcomings are artfully woven into the stuff of legends and his verbal skills are the basis of outdoor classics. Only the beginner will show up at camp and return early after avoiding all chores, claiming a muscle spasm which he covers with an ice pack. He fools no one. We all know that the rubber bottle is filled with ice cubes and gin.

While the amateur arrives with a hunting coat with the game pocket sewn shut so he won't have to carry his pheasant, the gentleman shows up with a jacket with no pockets at all, claiming they've been torn off by his pointer. He not only doesn't have to carry game, he will be given his shells by other members of the party.

I know you read outdoor writing for the vast quantities of expert advice it offers. But be that as it may, the greatest expert of all is the man who obviously can't do *anything*—then the real expert will step in and insist on doing it for him.

For example, most of this piece was actually written by Ed Zern.

Gene Hill

You're in
Trouble When . . .

Have you ever heard somebody say something to the effect, "Yeah, you know you're in trouble when. . .?" Sure you have. But, I've never heard anyone spout that concerning the outdoors. I've got a few of these, ALL related to the outdoors. You've been through them too, I'll bet. Listen up. You know you're in trouble when:

. . . Your partner's fly rod bows to the water just after you've consummated the 'five bucks on the biggest fish' bet.

. . . When a local gas station attendant gives you directions to a good grouse cover and ends his spiel with the words, "It's only 'bout a half mile from here."

. . . When the guy you bragged to about your shooting before the hunt uncases a custom-built Winchester Model 21.

. . . When you're so late from the evening duck shoot that your wife is waiting up for you—sitting on the garage floor where your car should be parked.

. . . When your wife spends too much time in the attic around your hunting clothes and then announces a garage sale.

. . . When your dog starts making strange sounds in the back seat of your partner's new car—and your partner that day is also your boss.

. . . When the new guy you promised to take hunting

asks you "What's this thing?" and he's pointing at his shotgun's safety. (Here is where you suddenly get sick and leave.)

. . . When your wife announces at a dinner party, "Oh, you men should go hunting with my husband. He knows ALL the best spots."

. . . When you take your camera and tripod out of the car, slip, and hear a loud noise—and you were able to avoid falling because the tripod helped you keep your balance.

. . . When the owner of the lodge you've driven 900 miles to fish from responds, "Well, heh, heh, it's like this . . ." when you ask how the fishing's been.

. . . When the new guy at deer camp feeds you his specialty he cooked up, waits until you're done eating, and then says, "You'll NEVER guess what you just ate."

. . . When the guy across from you at the deer camp card table bets the limit and then draws no cards.

Steve Smith

A Trapshooter's Confession

No poet will ever dedicate a lyric to the clay target, and I'm afraid that my trapshooting is as bad as my verse—or worse—but how I love the game! I grew up in that long lost era where children were seen and not heard. No right-thinking parent, surely not mine, ever deviated from the proven principle of "spare the rod and spoil the child," and they weren't much worried about our growing up maladjusted, either. So my introduction to clay-target shooting was working the trap and collecting the unbroken targets. No one ever considered letting me shoot. I never considered asking.

How I envied the shooters back in those days. The cool skill they exhibited with the single-barrel Foxes, Parkers, and Ithacas seemed to be to be the absolute epitome of grandeur. I know that I was a terrible wing shot myself, and I'm sure that was no little part of my awe.

One of the nicest things about old gun clubs is the row after row of sepia-colored photographs of the gunners in their buttoned-at-the-collar work shirts, the careful hair combs above the starched collars framing a serious set to the eyes that could seemingly shatter targets with a glance. (There's a picture of me and George Coe and Ken Gibson taken a year ago at a shoot and we all have our hats on sideways and look rather silly; it seems a mockery of the days when men were more serious about their shooting pastimes. Of course, we don't shoot as well, either.)

I shot my first trap at the kind of shoots that country gun clubs arrange to earn money. You paid fifty cents or a dollar and shot at ten targets. The prize was a chicken. (I seem to remember a preponderance of leather-skinned Rhode Island Reds. Somehow it always seemed fitting to shoot for something you could eat.) I don't think I ever shot ten straight— if anyone did he walked pretty tall and was whispered about at all the other shoots for the entire fall.

The trap was set up behind hay bales and scrap lumber and you could count on some pretty wild targets. No matter how badly you shot there was always some old buddy who'd say, "Well, meebe he can't hit them clay targets, but byjeezus you ought to see him when it's got feathers on it!" (if anybody said that about me, it was likely me).

If you showed up with a single-barrel or a Model 12 Winchester everybody talked about the "regular trap gun," no matter what it really was. The most common guns were the old side-by-sides: Lefevers, Trojan- and Vulcan-grade Parkers, Model 24 Winchesters, and the bottom-of-the-line LCs and Ithacas. They all had double triggers, extractors, and thirty-inch barrels and were sworn to be all full choke. And more than one was wired and taped together. Most of them kicked like hammers.

The shoots always had a "dead mark." You bought a square inch marked out on the back of an old movie poster with X in it from corner to corner. Someone shot at it, and the person whose square had the shot closest to the cross of the X won a turkey.

The ladies brought food, mostly cakes and pies, sold coffee and soda, and flirted with the men to get them to buy chances on the dead mark or to shoot another round of trap.

I found a shoot like that again last fall and foolishly turned up in my shooting jacket, with my two pair of shooting glasses. Although I knew one or two farmers there casually, I'm afraid, I was the center of all eyes as I uncased my trap gun. I was very well aware that I was almost the only man there with a real trap jacket and a real trap gun. Everybody else had on their work clothes and brought the gun they shot everything with. I paid my dollar and stepped up to the line. The trap was some kind of old, hand-fed job and threw the targets almost straight up in the air.

I knew they'd be hellishly hard to hit and was overwhelmed when I smoked the first five, six, and seven. Everybody else had missed one or two—and then I dropped three in a row. The winner had broken eight. "No smartass with his special gun and clothes is gonna come here and show us how to shoot," was the relieved general attitude when I walked off the line. I knew how I used to feel not too long ago and I must admit I agreed with them. It wouldn't have been fitting or right if I'd won.

I think my first registered trap shoot happened to be at the Grand American at Vandalia, Ohio—the Olympics of trapshooting. I just happened to be there and decided I wanted to shoot, so I borrowed a gun and shot. Mercifully, I've forgotten my score. But I do remember leaving with the firm belief that nobody is born that bad a shot, and with the firm conviction that I could learn if I only had my own trap gun. So shortly after that I became the owner of an old, nickel-steel Model 12. And, hat in hand, I turned up at a trap club I'd heard about and asked if I could shoot.

Like most trap clubs they couldn't have been more pleasant. I was even invited back—mostly because trapshooters are as full of advice as golfers and delight in finding a head as empty as mine that they can fill with advice and theories.

The terrible transition from a normal human being into a trapshooter is hell on a man's family. First off, you decide that the reason everybody shoots better than you do is that they have more odds and ends of equipment; shooting glasses, shooting gloves, shooting hats, shell cases, and eyeshades. All this is acquired in a great rush so you, too, can become an expert. I had my Model 12 restocked. I added a trigger shoe. I tuned the trigger. I still fumbled.

The answer was obvious: more guns. Guns came and went in graduated economic progression. The checkering became finer, the engraving more profuse—the scores stayed the same. No fortune seemed more fickle and alluring than 50 straight—or none seemingly less attainable. But at least I had finally gotten to the point where there were worse shooters. Not many, but some.

My bedside table was (and still is) littered with printed advice: Lee Braun's book on trap, Fred Missildine's book on trap, books on choke boring, books on wing shooting, Captain Bogardus and Purdey and Churchill and Etchen. Books that say hold a low gun, books that say hold the gun high. I've tried swinging through, pointing out and towing targets—in short, I know everything about the game. Too much, I guess, because I can never settle down and stick with one routine. I'm $\frac{1}{3}$ Etchen, $\frac{1}{3}$ Braun, and $\frac{1}{3}$ Missildine. And I guess the parts don't really fit together.

One of the alluring things about trap is that it's pretty much the same game of skill no matter what the degree of formality. You can fire above the straightaway and behind the right angles just as easily at the local volunteer fire department shoot as you can at Travers Island. And you can always find somebody better than you are on a given day, anyplace.

The thing that really intrigues me about trap is the endless variety of the shotguns. You can watch a squad take its place on the 16-yard line and see five different guns. The trapshooter never lived who doesn't believe that somewhere there is a trap gun that will solve his problems—and he'll never own it. This is the game for dreamers. With every box of fresh shells comes the idea that this may be the round when I really discover the secret, the little thing that a Dan Orlich knows that I don't—yet.

That's the nagging and elusive thing about trap, the so-near-but-yet-so-far mystery of the game. After all, it's not a question of strength or stamina or speed. It's not a question of being fat or thin or tall or short. Or even a man or woman. Or young or old. If you can break five in a row why can't you break 25? If you can break 25 why can't you continue through 100, and then 200? That's why we keep coming back.

I like trapshooters. I like the talk that floats around a gun club. I'll always feel a little tingle of excitement as I get ready to call for my first birds—and the pleased surprise when I break it. This is about the only sport I know where the winner is usually more embarrassed than the loser, and offers as many excuses.

Trap has given me some of the most pleasant times and some of my closest friends. And that's what it's all about.

I forgot who was remarking about the laws of compensation and went on to say ". . . even take ice, for example, the poor gets theirs in the winter and the rich gets theirs in the summer." I have a wife and two daughters, and trapshooting's made me conveniently hard of hearing. You couldn't say that about golf! (I just remembered who said the bit about ice: Bat Masterson.)

Gene Hill

Outdoor Tips

Have you ever seen those sections in the sporting magazines that give little tips to make the outdoor world more pleasant and productive?

Things like: "Carry extra dry matches in your hatband so they'll stay dry," or something like that?

Well, the guys who write those things haven't been around much. All these tips assume that you've thought of everything else except the small stuff.

For you and me, it's another story. Here are what I call Outdoor-Tips-I-Wish-I'd-Had-Before-I-Went:

If you are going into a marshy area to fish, make sure your pal hasn't replaced the bug dope with colored sugar water.

If you are alone on an outing and a sudden storm comes up, don't head for shelter in a creek culvert.

When told by the locals that the stream is only three feet deep, don't believe them.

When the man at the canoe livery tells you the trip takes only four hours, and you'll be done by nightfall, consider him a liar.

Your chances of picking a non-poisonous mushroom in the fall are about 12 zillion to one.

Getting interested in outdoor photography is only slightly less expensive than buying a rapid transit system for the State of California.

Plan a fishing trip, make all arrangements, then go a week earlier or a week later, because that's when they'll be biting, certainly not the week you've planned.

The dam you are fishing below will invariably open the flood gates about the time you hook into a 15-pound steelhead.

Your dog which you've bragged about to your buddies will suddenly take up car sickness, but only if it's the buddies car.

Consider all weathermen to be brothers under the skin to the canoe livery guys.

Remember that all fences are either barbed, electrified, or both. Try to remember this before you get half way over.

The gun you really want will be all of the following: too expensive, the wrong gauge, poor fit, too heavy. Also remember that you'll end up buying it anyway.

Finally, remember that farmers who willingly give you permission to hunt know the following that you don't: They have a large bull in the back 40, there are no birds on the property, you'll park your car in the wrong spot, pocket the keys, and have to run back two miles so he can move his tractor. Good luck!

Steve Smith

Figuring It Out

One of the assets that accrues to the outdoorsman is the number of excuses you can rummage up to buy another parka, another shooting coat, another pair of camouflage suspenders, and so on. The old-time catalogs used to list this nifty stuff in their prosaic fashion. A size was a number, in inches, that roughly corresponded to your waist or chest and the color was described simply, but accurately, as gray or brown or red or whatever. Very simple, very functional.

But times change and personal artistry must have its moment. The good people who write catalog copy had to improve on all this. *Improve* is not my word, it's theirs.

Not long ago I was eyeing a rather well-designed parka in one of the more popular catalogs. I didn't really need another parka but this one had a couple of more pockets and some new kind of insulation and I imagined that I might reflect a pretty neat image with it thrown carelessly over my shoulders. I could justify it on the other hand by wearing it under my fishing vest as well as seeing it perfectly suitable to wear on one of my social outings, such as going to the post office to pick up my mail. All in all, a versatile garment.

I went down to the small print where they hide the vital statistics and found that it was offered in two colors: mushroom and slate. I don't consider myself a mycologist, but I do know that mushrooms come in gray, white, tan, a muddy brown, and I think some have a rather pinkish cast. I am not a geologist either, but I have enough slate around the farm to know that it had it more than one hue. The decision was more than I could handle, so I passed. But had I decided on slate, my next guessing game was M, L, or XL. No comforting numbers. Bitter and costly experience has taught me that one man's XL is another man's L. Too risky.

Boots and shoes come, nowadays, in different widths: narrow, medium, and wide. My foot, properly shod, requires what is known as a "B" in the better shops. I feel better about ordering something with a specific sound to it. Being a medium is about as specific and flattering as being a PFC. What size is medium? What size is average?

You don't see a shotgun barrel marked "medium." You don't see a fly line marked with that ultimate illusion "one size fits all." You don't buy a box of 7mm Magnums that says the bullet weight is somewhere between 160 and 165 grains. Shotgun shells don't come in "petite" or "tall," they come in a plain, understandable 4, 6, or $7\frac{1}{2}$.

One place where they get very specific is the price: $49.95 plus $2.00 postage and $1.50 insurance. You'll note they don't say, "Send in what you think it's worth or whatever you can spare at the moment." I expect that you've noticed that if you want a duck coat, for example, in a size XXL, that this is another $5.00 or so. But if you want one for the Queen Bee who is a hefty 118 pounds, they don't mark it down to even the whole thing out.

Not long ago I was shopping for a new dress shirt. I found the $16\frac{1}{2} \times 35$ pile and they had one unwrapped so you could try it on. I was barely able to force my arms through the sleeves, the cuff wouldn't button and when the front was fastened, breathing was obviously out of the question. I asked the salesperson if the same thing had happened to $16\frac{1}{2} \times 35$ shirt that had happened to the 2" × 4" board. He said that the shirt I had on was a European cut; I needed a label that did not say "trim" or "athlete" or any of the other words

that let manufacturers hedge a few inches off the garment
in question. He said I was "full sized." You bet your medium-
width, slate-colored boots I am!

I am not a quarrelsome person and aside from the trap
and skeet scores, I'm of normal or thereabouts intelligence.
I do have certain likes and dislikes, believe in the Golden
Rule, and expect a straight answer to a simple question.
While I am amused by certain fads like wristwatches that
require both hands to get the time, philosophical credos on
what used to be called underwear, camouflage shoelaces,
and belt buckles that are as big as saucers, I hang on to the
old live-and-let-live concepts. I just don't hold with wild
cards in poker or guessing games when I need a new chamois
shirt in tan; not huckleberry or mist.

One of the great things about our English language is
that it can be most precise. But you have to learn the vocabulary of whomever it is that you're dealing with. When a
Texan says the green stuff he's pouring on his steak is a
"little bitey," you know enough to pass it by or suffer the
consequences of either your bravado or ignorance. When
you're told by a Georgian that the next quail cover is "just
a piece," you had better start looking for the truck unless
your attachment to the infantry is a lot stronger than mine.
"A little choppy" to a Florida fisherman immediately con-
jures up headlines in the paper about "Yankee Fisherman
Feared Lost!" If your Maine guide says, "There might be a
bird here and there," be prepared for one of the best shooting
days of your life. We've all learned that the eight-pound bass
runs about 6–6½; that the 300 yard shot will pace out around
220, and that "about half a box of shells" to the dove hunter
means 35 or 40. When a duck hunter tells his wife he'll be
home "a little after dark" she doesn't start to worry until
about 10:30. This is day-to-day stuff for must of us.

Our hunting and fishing crowd tends to avoid the direct
answer, preferring to leave a couple of options open or a
little room for personal interpreation. That's fine by me since
I know the rules of the game. When you ask how my new
Labrador pup is coming along and I say, "She's nice and

headstrong, just the kind I like to work with," you know that so far I haven't gotten her to come when she's called, she won't sit and stay, and spends plenty of time up on the good furniture. Or when a buddy tells you that his pointer isn't broken to flush and he'd just as soon leave it that way, you know that there's a dog you won't see more than five minutes out of an hour.

A lot of this depends on who's around during the conversation. If it's a wife and you're discussing a new gun that he says was a steal, you leave it at that; friends never use numbers in front of each other's wives unless it's inches of trout or a quantity of ducks or the hour you're going to pick him up. Wives are born with a built-in computer anyway. A woman who thinks that "Purdey" is the way a Texan might describe a beauty queen will instinctively know within ninety-eight cents what you shelled out for that shotgun. I don't know how they know, I just know that they do. I have a couple of secret methods for adding the odd gun to my pathetic collection which I dare not reveal in public. But basically, it's easier to upgrade than it is to add a new number to what you already have. Just be sure that if you do that the guns look alike—single barrels for single barrels and so on. You could, for example, go from a 1100 to a Perazzi trap gun, but not to an O/U Browning.

It's a good idea to avoid as much gun talk around or with your wife as you can. Of course, if she's a shooter, as mine is, this can be exceedingly difficult, not to say expensive. All you do here, as I have had to do, is convince her that she shoots a lot better with a stock that's $14\frac{1}{2}$ inches long and hope for the best.

There's been a spate of odd vocabulary books. *How To Talk Texan* is one that comes to mind. It ought to be easy to put such a volume together for the outdoor set. I've already mentioned a few, others like *LUCK: What Your Opponent Has in a Shoot Off; SECOND HAND: Description of a New Gun You Had Custom-Made; CHOKE: One of the Reasons You Didn't Win the Shoot Off; TRAP LOAD: Your Condition After Staying Too Long at the Gun Club;* I'm sure you could come up with a dozen more in a little time. But to get back where we came in, if anyone out there knows how many inches in *medium* or what color *mushroom* is, I'd like to include them in one of my columns as a public service.

Gene Hill

Calling Ducks

U lysses S. Grant once remarked that he only knew two tunes. One of them was "The Star Spangled Banner" and the other one wasn't. And compared to me, General Grant was a musical prodigy. Be that as it may, I am getting my hands on as many duck and goose calls as I can. I intend to learn to call waterfowl even if in the process I offend every ear in the country—and I just might. Even my Labradors have started to slink into the dark recesses of their kennel, and the rest of the world around the farm becomes dumb and silent as I tune up my "highball" and "feeding chatter" out behind the barn.

I thought I had a goose call working pretty good—and I did except the one I had down to an acoustical fine point was the danger call, a single, piercing honk that I can reproduce with such fidelity that no goose ever hearing it has stopped climbing until he has reached his maximum altitude, which I believe is somewhere in the neighborhood of 28,000 feet.

My duck calls, on the other hand, are such a curious combination of unnatural sharps and flats that more than one mallard has succumbed and warily circled over my blind, no doubt only out of an incredible aural curiosity rather than what I hoped would be a verbal promise of feathered companionship, great food, or a torrid love affair.

Like most of us, I tend to quickly shift any of my own

personal shortcomings over the area of blaming them on faulty equipment and go out and buy something new. Right now I have four different calls, two duck and two geese— and a pintail and widgeon whistle that I won't count, because I haven't gotten around to working on that yet. I'm not sure if anyone makes an instrument that can begin to compensate for the fact that I'm about as tone deaf as a post—but I'm trying them all. And to give myself the pat on the back that I truly deserve, without out-and-out bragging, after only a few months of practice I have come up with a very recognizable version of both "Mary Had a Little Lamb" and "Silent Night" on the harmonica.

There are few things I enjoy more than waterfowling and all that goes with it. The deep envy that I radiate when the weather-tanned guide nonchalantly hauls some birds down within range with a few casual notes on his call has become more than I can control. When I'm out behind the barn practicing to the sheep I constantly have this mental image of myself, dressed in hip boots, my old and battered but very distinguished ducking cap pulled just slightly down over my eyes, my three-inch magnum 1100 casually tucked in the crook of my left arm and about four assorted calls strung around my neck. My weather-tanned face warily scans the cold and shallow light of just dawn on a real weather-making morning. My experienced eyes pick out a small flock of ducks— still so far away that the other men in the blind have no idea of their presence.

"Blacks," I say casually. "About two miles off, twelve hundred feet high, at eleven o'clock."

"How can you tell?" ask the greenhorns with me in the blind.

"Count the wingbeats," I whisper, and start to finger the Olt call I favor for distance work.

"He thinks he can call those birds in," followed by not too muffled laughter, comes from behind me in the blind. I turn, silence the chattering with a scowl and put my call to my lips. In spite of the incredible volume, there issues forth a sound so ancient, so pure, so wild, so magically entrancing that even before the lead black starts to turn I can hear the quick snapping as the gunners check the safeties and the rustling of heavy gunning clothes as the men instinctively crouch lower in the blind.

I smile to myself and shift to another call, a gleaming masterpiece made from soft glowing Osage orange. A subtle series of chuckles follows that sounds like a hen mallard reading the menu of a duck's version of the 21 Club. The flock is swiftly closing in and is about to turn upwind and scatter in the blocks. I give the signal for the other guns to stand and take their shots. And after all have missed, I rise and pull a pair of drakes, stone cold, at 55 or 60 yards. Then without a word, I send my perfectly trained retriever into the bay. My weather-tanned face permits itself a slight but manly grin of satisfaction as I turn to the other men and promise that I'll call the next bunch in a little closer—if they'd like. I bring out my pintail whistle and start to work a flock that they have yet to spot, as the Labrador brings in the second duck and puts it in my hand.

So this fall if you should happen to see a weathered ducker in hip boots, a nicely flavored cap pulled down just slightly over his eyes, an automatic magnum tucked in the crease of his left arm, a perfectly mannered Lab at his side and enough calls strung around his neck to make him look like a pipe organ, stop and say "hello." It's me imitating a duck hunter.

Gene Hill

Toby

The Smith family is presently being raised by a puppy, a new experience for all of us, particularly since that pup is an English pointer with the blood of grouse-hunting canine royalty flowing in his veins.

His name is Toby, short for "October," the favorite month of a bird dog and the man he owns. He's 11 weeks old, has feet the size of a cub bear, and legs that grow, like an aspen cut, almost as you watch. Those legs aren't cooperating right now. They don't really go the direction Toby wants them to go, so he does a lot of falling down and running into things. The things he runs into, by the way, are inside. I finally won the battle with Sweetwife to get a bird dog and make him an inside pet as well as a hunting companion. I have to tell you, the going was tough.

Sweetwife thinks that houses are for people, and kennels are for dogs. She worried about shed fur and what happens behind the potted rubber tree when nobody's looking. But, after a few days of being around the puppy, Sweetwife has had her heart stolen by another male—this one with big liver-colored spots—that doesn't quite come when he's called like I'd like him to.

Dick Neal, a real nice guy who works for the Ruffed Grouse Society, has been teaching me how to train Toby. Dick only tells me what I should know at that particular time.

He knows that if I knew more, I'd try to push things (Dick's from West Virginia, so he says "poosh") and I'd botch it up. He's right, naturally, so I have to play along.

I got one of my biggest thrills when Toby was nine weeks old and I dangled a grouse wing in front of him on a line suspended from one of my son's fishing poles. He chased the wing twice, and I jerked it away, just like Dick said I should. On the third try, Toby ambled up to the wing and snapped into a foot-up-tail-high-bring-shivers-down-your-spine-honest-to-golly point. My phone bill that week was about 80 bucks as I called all my family and buddies to let them know that maybe, just this once, I'd have something that isn't a cast-off or second rate, like my hunting clothes and other stuff.

Well, Toby hasn't really disappointed me a bit, but the family has. Toby has become the focal point of attention from the Smith tribe, and he's soaking it up. He sleeps indoors, and holds court perched on the cushion of what had been considered, heretofore, "Dad's chair."

The best tidbits from the table go into his growing maw, and he gets patted, petted, and played with nearly nonstop. Frankly, I don't think he knows he's a dog. I think he thinks he's people. Apparently that comes from the mistress of the house holding him in her lap while she watches television. In fact, he's lately taken to giving me a haughty look when I try to coax him off that lap for a little rough-and-tumble on the living room floor. He looks at me like I've got two heads, so after awhile I get to feeling embarrassed and go sit down and he goes back to sleep.

He's also raising hob with the kids. Last week he broke up a rainy day Monopoly game by stealing the money from the bank and the deed to Boardwalk. He steamed out of the back bedroom, trailing blue 20-dollar bills and towing a gaggle of kids demanding that his miserable hide be tacked to the tool shed—but not really meaning it.

As he grows, there may be some problems. I have scrupulously avoided making public any photographs of full-

grown male pointers. It's best to wait a bit, or—better yet—
wait for time and Purina to have their collective effect slowly,
so the shock won't be too great.

So, for right now, we are taking walks in the woods
where Toby brings me half rotted sticks and dead leaves,
and spends time tripping over logs and his own feet and my
own feet. Raising a pup is fun, and raising him with people
you love and he will come to love, is even more fun. Who
knows, someday next season—probably late next season—
he might even point a grouse. That's when he finds out his
most meaningful lesson in life: Master can't shoot.

Steve Smith

Another New Gun

I was just sort of talking out loud the other night, to myself and Tip, the old Labrador who understands such things, about how much I'd like to own a new gun. *"What new gun?"* my wife threw in from over some mending. "I thought you owned at least one of everything—no, I don't mean that—I mean one of everything and *two sets of barrels!"* So I patiently went through the fact that seeing as how we live in an advanced, international era of technology there were several sorts of new guns around from countries not as yet represented in my gun closet—A fact that I didn't feel was fair since they're the ones that need the most encouragement. She started reciting from memory that, for a fact, I owned guns from Australia, Germany, England, and for all she knew about what I had hidden away in the barn there might be stuff from Albania, Outer Mongolia, or the Baffin Islands, and so on.

It was quite a while before I restored any kind of calm. You know how some women are when they get the bit in their teeth over hardware you can't use to clean rugs with or cut grass. But I wanted to enlighten her so she wouldn't embarrass me in front of my shooting buddies so I hung in there until she paused for breath somewhere between Tierra del Fuego and Micronesia. I went on, patiently, that there were a couple of guns around now that came from Italy. The land of Michelangelo and the Caesars had finally gotten around to exporting something a fellow could come to grips with besides movie stars. "How much does it cost?" she asked me. I said that I hadn't even said what it *was*. She said that it obviously was some kind of super trap gun and she didn't care *what* it was, but she did care about *how much* it was. I said that it was a new Perazzi, that Ithaca imported to help out the balance of trade relations between the United States and Italy and that Ithaca probably lost money on it, et cetera, et cetera, since it was more of a good will gesture than anything else, et cetera.

She had, by now, quit the mending and was paying more than polite attention. She asked "how much?" a couple more times and finally I said that I thought the Perazzi that I kind of leaned toward, the MX 8 model, could be picked up for around $1500. She let that sit on her mind a minute or so and then kind of leaned back and smiled and commenced to get back to the sewing. I figured that was the logical end of the discussion and went back to rubbing Tippy under her chin to make her smile. I had my fingers under Tip's collar and she was beaming away when the voice of my conscience put the mending down again and said, "Only $1500? I don't see why not because, obviously, you really need it. We can probably get about $200 by selling the rugs, another $500 for the furniture—that's $700. My two old winter coats are worth about $10 apiece and if we cut out the riding lessons for the kids, sell my grandmother's silver service. . . ." Well, she went on until she had stripped the house, impoverished the kids, and was reduced to wearing feed bags while she went to welfare for food coupons . . . but she finally got up the mental $1500.

I waited until she had finished and said to the dog, "See that, Tip? You aren't the only smart female in this house that knows you can't shoot trap with any living room rug!"

"Yes," she continued, "if we really did have an extra $2000 we didn't know what to do with, I wouldn't mind seeing you have your fourth or fifth really fine, first-class gun." I reminded her that it only costs $1500 for a Perazzi. "And with the other $500 left over I'd like to have a really fine, first-class winter coat." I was about to ask what in the world she needed another winter coat for when I felt old Tip reach up and tug my hand. I understood what she meant and shut up.

Gene Hill

Tackling The
Tackle Box

In the middle of winter, one of the small pleasures that I often enjoy is when I start to clean out my tackle box from last summer, getting ready for the next.

Summers are great, winters are lousy, so by working on my fishing stuff, I manage to psych myself into believing that summer is only days away, instead of months.

I sat down the other day to do just that, and found out some rather suprising things. I found out that my older boy, Chris, had managed to glom onto most of my good stuff and like a pack rat, had left his castoffs in return. I found a box of dry flies had been swapped for a chewed on deer hair bug I'd given him once. I found that he had liberated a pair of surface bass lures in exchange for a pack of snelled hooks, and a 25 cent fish stringer now occupied the place I usually set aside for my spare spinning reel.

With the switches finally unswitched, I was ready to see what I could do about the tackle box. As always, the sorting brought back a flood of memories from the past season, some of which I'll pass on to you.

I remembered the day I slunk low enough to fish for trout with worms. Pieces of long-deceased nightcrawlers were stuck to the bottom of the tackle box. The Chippewa Indians had a word for this condition—Yucch! I also remembered that I hadn't caught anything that day.

I found a half-used pouch of pipe tobacco in the bottom, a grim reminder of the day I leaned over the boat to net a bass for my partner and opened my yap to give him advice on playing the fish. Exit the pipe for which the tobacco was intended. There's probably a message there which I'll ignore.

I ran across what was left of the finest brown drake fly I'd ever seen tied. I say remains because I got desperate and used the fly—intended for trout—on a buster smallmouth and all I got was exercise and a busted fly. Gotta get some more. I also found a picture of my ever present partner, Chris, with his first smallmouth, a fine, chunky fish which I somehow ham-handled into the boat where we both pounced on it.

Finally, I found the map a local guy drew for me showing me how to get to a deserted lake far from the beaten path down a nameless creek. There was no lake, and I'll bet he's still laughing. I'll have to find him this year and lie through my teeth about the great fishing I found, just to watch him squirm.

If you aren't doing anything right now, go get your tackle box and open it up and try to remember what happened to you this past year. Then, vow not to repeat any of it this year.

Steve Smith

$6,537.50

There are in life a lot of phrases that sound magnificent and truthful but in fact carry the real burden concealed—much like the iceberg. Among the more familiar are marriage vows, New Year's resolutions, fishing stories, poker winnings, and estimates of how much it will cost to go shooting. Put another way, "There are lies and *damn* lies."

If you are among the many that have not so far ventured to embrace either trap or skeet, let me give you a glimpse as to what lies under the surface—like the murderous part of the iceberg.

You ask your buddy who sports "25 straight" patches over his imported, custom-made, silk shooting jacket "How much does it cost to shoot skeet?" He, in truth, says (especially if his wife is in earshot; remember, wives are *always* in earshot), "Oh, clay targets run to about a nickel apiece . . . a dollar twenty-five a round. Plus shells, of course, brings it to about three-and-a-half bucks."

You, a sweet, white-robed innocent, figure three or four times three-and-a-half bucks—not an unlikely sport. It can be swung. And indeed it could, if what your buddy said was even up to being a half-truth.

Here is a short summary of what you must add to the $3.50 it costs to shoot a round of trap or skeet: shooting jacket, shooting glasses, shooting gloves, and shooting hat. (You think you have these or can make do? Wrong. You will feel like the first gal at the beach to show up in a topleess bathing suit.) There are in fact, shooting shirts, shooting ties, shooting pants, shooting belts, shooting shoes, and socks. But these come later. You *must* play poker, gin rummy, or pinochle between rounds. You will probably lose. Your turn to buy a round will come when everyone has just switched from beer to Jack Daniels. They might be doubles. You will be badgered into membership in the NSSA, ATA, NRA, PITA, one or more wildlife organizations, and tickets to the next police function.

As I said, this is only a superficial summary. The details vary and are really not important; they depend somewhat on local customs. What you should know is that the grand total to shoot a round of skeet or trap will amount to roughly $6,537.50. But don't be disheartened. Look at the positive side—don't think of it as expensive, think of all the things that cost more: an African safari, a Rolls-Royce, a matched pair of Purdeys, or a Mexican divorce.

Gene Hill

Bartlett and the
Grouse Hunter

This fella John Bartlett, who is quoted often because he quoted often, had some words about grouse hunters that he picked up from other folks. Too bad for him he didn't know it—could have made a ton of money selling the book to grouse and woodcock buffs.

I was breezing through *Bartlett's Familiar Quotations* a few years ago (which is sort of like "breezing through" *The Rise and Fall of The Roman Empire*, when it hit me that most of these people were talking about us—you and me.

For example, when Will Rogers said that he "never met a man I didn't like," then he never met my pal Charlie, a lawyer who, besides bragging about his shooting, also had the nerve to once go five-for-five on grouse. Haven't heard the end of it yet, nor am I likely to. Seems Charlie hit a string of easy straightaways over good points in open cover and the law of averages, after years of missing these shots, finally reached up and smacked him upside his thick skull and he lucked into five birds with that many right barrels. Shakespeare (by way of Bartlett) had something to say about guys like him when he said, "First we kill all the lawyers. . . ." Shakespeare must have known Charlie because the thought has crossed my mind a time or two when he introduced himself to somebody when I'm along with the words, "Ever tell you how I went five-for-five on grouse?"

In fact, Bartlett kind of got me in a jam with my wife

the tag end of last season. Seems she saw me slipping out the back with the old double and young dog to head for the woodcock covers and she started giving it to me about the storm windows. Naturally, I quoted Samuel Johnson with, "I am very fond of the company of ladies. I like their beauty, I like their delicacy, I like their vivacity, and I like their silence." That went over about as well as you'd imagine.

And Johnson also had something to say about my pal Harvey who always claims he moves, "40 grouse and 30 woodcock" about every time out. Johnson said: "Round numbers are always false."

Speaking of the Storm and Strife, as I was a little bit ago, Robert Browning knew the ribbing she gives me about coming home skunked every now and again and how the fear of her barbs tends to make me shoot a little straighter on occasion. He said, "What most moved him was a certain meal of beans." See what I mean?

In the process of trying to cross an electric cattle fence with wet shooting pants last year, I was given to quoting Mark Twain when he said, "The right word is a powerful agent. Whenever we come upon one of those . . . the results are electrically prompt." I can tell you, the "right word" in that case was not found in Bartlett's!

I introduced my aforementioned pal Harvey to the joys of grouse hunting a few seasons ago. Harvey let on that he was really a great bird hunter, but five minutes into the first cover and I could see the game was new to him. So, like a sport, I took him under my wing, taught him how to shoot, and made a bird hunter out of him.

Now, he often shoots better than I do, (rarely, though), buys better guns, and drinks better whiskey. Reminds me, again, of Twain who said, "If you pick up a starving dog and make him prosperous, he will not bite you. This is the principal difference between a dog and a man."

But, when it became apparent that Harvey was also stealing my covers because he hunts during the week and I on weekends, I sort of got even. I stopped over to show him a limit of woodcock (because he had never seen a limit before) on a weekend last fall, and Harv, of course asks me where I got 'em.

Pulling myself up tall, I think of Twain again, and—in my very best voice—say to him, "I was gratified to be able to answer promptly, and I did. I said I didn't know."

Steve Smith

How Many Guns Are Enough?

Dear Ms. Johnson:
Thank you very much for your pleasant letter. I always enjoy hearing from ladies, and of course, I'm delighted to try to answer your question—as I believe I can see the situation that lies behind it.

You ask me, "How many guns do you have?" And I suspect that you feel the man in your life is reaching a level that you, in your innocence, feel is sufficient, or perhaps overabundant.

Let me answer your question first from a more realistic angle, the angle that I, like most men, regretfully have to face every day of my life. What are the guns that I *don't* have!

I do not own, nor have I had the opportunity to own—which goes without saying—a good side-by-side .470 double rifle. I often bring this up at home when my own wife remarks that I seem a bit peckish or morose. Her predictable response is that I don't have any earthly use for a .470 double, a .500 double or a .577 double. She doesn't have any use for a profile like Raquel Welch either, but that doesn't mean she wouldn't like it. Suppose someone asked me to go to Africa, what would I say? Suppose, worse yet, that a guest asked to see my double rifle, assuming that any right-thinking sportsman would own one, and I have to stand there shifting uneasily from one foot to another making up very transparent excuses like, "It's back in London having the sears hardened." I can only compare it to a man going through life without a good blue suit; it's that basic.

Worse yet, I'm probably the only person in the group I regularly associate with that doesn't own a .30-06. Most of my friends own several, luckily, and they would never think of asking about mine any more than they would insist on seeing my marriage license. (I assume your husband has both.)

I do not even own a .243, a .22 Hornet (near the top of my must list!), a .300 H&H, or even the common 7mm magnum. I don't mean to sound like Oliver Twist pleading for more porridge, nor do I mean to imply that since your man has, very likely, all of these and more, that he is among the blessed. I am merely stating the unpleasant facts—there are people like that, you know, and I fear I am one of "those."

I could go on, but rather than reduce you to a state of uncontrolled pity where you start sneaking me duplicates from your husband's basic collection, let me shift you away from the sordid confession that I have no wherewithal to collect rhino, nothing for 300-yard antelope, no match target piece, and I am drawing zero in the area that my friend Tony Dyer from Nairobi would classify as a decent "medium rifle."

Far worse is my assembly (a stroke of humor here in that word) of basic shotguns. Let us begin by saying that if I were invited tomorrow to partake in a round of skeet involving the .410 or the 28-gauge I would have to plead a sick headache or say that I had just finished washing my hair.

Even as the 12th of August comes near, I must refuse to open my mail or answer the phone. The 12th, as you know, is the traditional opening day of grouse shooting in Scotland, and as you might have already guessed, I have nothing that remotely resembles the matched pair of 12 bores that are as mandatory for a gentleman gunner as a heather-shade pair of shooting knickers.

I could too easily go on, but I'm sure you have your problems and don't need a recitation of mine. You might fairly say that I'm dodging your question, which in a way I am, but there is a second, and more realistic answer.

A close reading of much of shooting's modern literature reveals the fact that only two men in the world have enough guns. One is a Middle East potentate who patterns his Purdeys on the rear door of a special Rolls-Royce made especially for this function. (It's a fine way to get a two-dimensional look at a shot pattern, as you can closely simulate the speed of flight of most game birds and check the effect of density as well as the length of effective shot stringing.)

The other is a bearded writer for an outdoor publication, who will be instantly identified by merely mentioning he is a worse shot than I am.

Guns, like love, cannot be measured with numbers. It's common knowledge to the student of modern sociology that the more guns a man owns the more happily married he tends to be.

I believe that the divorce rate of men who own more than one double rifle, or sidelock shotgun, in a high grade of course, is virtually nil. This is because today's extremely intelligent and sensitive liberated woman has discovered that a highly engraved Holland or Churchill, as a love token, has proven to quickly dry the tears of the most deeply hurt husband.

In my own case, when I embraced the common twins, youth and poverty, my wife set out our meager holiday dinners around a table whose centerpiece was a cleverly arranged motif of red and green 2¾ No. 8 trap loads, knowing that such a little gift would be far more cheering to my humble spirit than the more perishable and overly feminine flowers or fruit.

I'm sure that if you read between the lines, you'll find that the common term "shotgun wedding" has its real origin in a far different context than used today. Let's hope that the original meaning returns to warm our customs.

I, for one, still believe in the traditional dowry. And, since I have a brace of daughters, I pass up no opportunity to pick up another gun to enhance their chances of "good marriages" when the time comes. They seem perfectly willing to forego the shallow and passing need for new shoes and warm clothes knowing that their father is thinking ahead for their more important welfare in the future. And I know that there are a lot of fathers out there just like me. There'll be at least a dozen at any trap club, come any Sunday, making sure that their future sons-in-law will get shotguns that they know will please them, because they've used it and used it often.

I hope, in my circuitous way, I have been of some help to you. Let me remind you that the average outdoorsman is a very sensitive man. He does not want to embarrass his wife and family by going off on an elk hunt, let's say, unless he has a good .270, a .7mm Magnum, or a decent .375. Nor should we be misled by the fact that he shoots trap with a 4-grade Ithaca single barrel—what happens at the gun club when the fellows try to cajole him into a round of doubles? Does he beg off, saying that he forgot to bring the cashmere jacket his wife bought him for doubles, or does he snap open the brass locks of a top-grain leather trunk case and bring forth a high-grade over-and-under with "To G.A.H. from M.E.M." engraved on the receiver? Is he a well-appreciated husband or just another beast of burden? I leave that to you, my gentle reader.

May you happily look forward to the day when you can paraphrase the famous couplet of Elizabeth Barrett Browning: "How do I love thee? Let me count the guns. . . ."

Gene Hill

Letter to the
Pipe Maker

Dear Mr. Wilson:
As per your advertisement, printed media blitz, and the guarantee that accompanied the enclosed pipe, I am returning this item for refund. It has not "withstood punishment" as your advertising indicated that it would, and I want my money back—Pronto!

If you will take a good look at the pipe, you will notice some of the battle scars incurred during the course of pursuing—with the pipe—my favorite outdoor activities: grouse and woodcock hunting.

Now, everybody knows that grouse and woodcock hunters wear old felt hats, shoot smoothed-by-the-years old doubles, and smoke pipes. It wouldn't hardly be fitting if the pipe weren't included, right? So, looking for a pipe to finish out the wardrobe (I already had the hat and gun), I happened upon your model. I was looking for a workmanlike, straight-stemmed unit, and your offering looked nice. So, I sent you a check and the pipe arrived as you promised. After that, things tapered off right away.

The year that I owned the pipe and used it was marked by my usual misfortune and fooling around. In fact, this pipe makes a pretty good calendar of the events that marked that year. Since I am an average grouse and woodcock hunter, I can't see how you can have any choice but to make good on your claims.

For example, the large depressions near the end of the stem of the pipe mark my attempts at teaching my pointer pup the word "whoa." When you get a high-powered hunting dog, the line between genuis and knotheadedness in the dog is a thin one, indeed. I'd be following the dog, he'd point, I'd croon, "whooooooooooa," the bird would break, and Knucklehead was after him like he was shot from a cannon. Naturally, I'd scream, turn red, the veins would stand out in my neck, and I'd grit my teeth—I mean, what bird hunter wouldn't? Well, your pipe only minutely interfered with the gritting process hence the dents which correspond perfectly with my incisors and part of a bicuspid. Seems like a pipe should be able to withstand some dog training.

And the bowl, which you advertised as being, "ever-dry," was anything but. If you can bear it, take a sniff of the bowl and tell me it doesn't, if you dare, smell like a cesspool. That happened when I was crossing a stagnant little stream deep in Muckraker Swamp after woodcock. I was engaged, at the time, in doing the Mossy Rock Shuffle and lost the pipe from my mouth. More specifically, inertia held the pipe suspended in space where my mouth used to be after I took the Shuffle to its usual conclusion. I also lost my gun, some shells, a dog whistle, and a bologna sandwich. I recovered the gun and pipe and gave 'em both a shot of Hoppe's No. 9. Worked great on the gun; didn't do a thing for the pipe.

And, with all due respect, don't you think that a sportsman's pipe should be able to withstand a little distilled spirits? Take a look at yours—hell, the varnish came off!

That happened at grouse camp during the usual poker game before the opener. I had aces full, and I knew Crazy Charlie was holding a small straight. I bet the pot way up to a buck-and-a-half, and was waiting to raise Charlie. Charlie doesn't know if I'm bluffing or not until I reach over and set your pipe in a glass of Jack-and-branch. When I leap up to save the pipe, I screech something like, "Just when I get a full house, this happens!"

Charlie folds and the only money on the table is what I

bet plus the ante—big deal. If I had confidence in your pipe, I could have pretended I was "sweetening the bowl" with liquor and it was all planned. As it was, I look like I'm panicky because I have a good hand and the sucker slips away. Thereoughttabealaw.

Finally, your pipe has a stem and design that make it impossible to hold comfortable on the left side of my mouth while hunting—the right feels better. I'm right-handed. Know what happens when the best chance for a double all year comes up, you throw the gun to your shoulder, and the pipe is there? You get to say all kinds of things that your wife won't let you say when the kids are around, that's what.

So, please refund the entire purchase price of 89 cents immediately and we shall part only adversaries, not enemies.

Sincerely,
Steve Smith

Steve Smith

The Trip

As the readers of this book are no doubt aware, grouse and woodcock hunters are a cut above the average human, given to quoting Shakespeare, donating to the local opera company, and supporting the work of struggling young artists. Comparing them to pheasant hunters is like comparing the finest imported scotch with a can of beer.

Come, then, on a typical woodcock hunt with two such sterling personages to watch the drama of the chase unfold in all its magnificent splendor.

The time is mid-October, the season of the gods. The place, Michigan's Lower Peninsula—some of the best ruffed grouse and woodcock territory found anywhere on the planet. The cast of characters include Mark Sutton (M), his pointer, Dinah (known as Dog) and myself. I have chosen to record this episode just as it happened, with no attempt to embellish. I let the record stand for itself. All events are true, with times noted for verification purposes.

6:02 a.m.—M arrives at house driving his shooting car. Name of vehicle is derived from condition of clutch, engine, and transmission, all of which are, indeed, shot. Car—a 1954 Chevy—awakens several neighbors because it has not seen a muffler since the spring of 1959.

6:05 a.m.—Dog bounds from car and evacuates on Self's prize roses. M chuckles good naturedly at the antics of his animal, while Self calls down the wrath of gods on both M and his playful compadre. With this ritual completed, all leave for the northern Michigan shooting grounds.

7:15 a.m.—Arriving at the first cover of the day, we disembark from car. Our clothes carry the odor of exhaust fumes from the shooting car. Self promptly closes thumb in breech of fine, side-by-side 20-gauge double. M laughs with such enthusiasm that standing upright becomes impossible for him, and I take solace in the fact that M is now wet from rolling convulsively in the frosty grass. I curse the immortal soul of M for such frivolity. For good measure, I also curse 20 gauge.

8:12 a.m.—After missing four straight woodcock and a grouse, I finally connect on a rising woodcock. Dog, which has flawlessly retrieved all three of M's birds (taken with three shots), calmly finds and eats this bird, including head and bill. I am wild with rage; M is wild with hysteria brought on by inability to take in oxygen fast enough to support peals of laughter. I curse Dog with vocabulary usually reserved for Nazi war criminals and child molesters. Dog licks chops and eagerly demands that we continue hunt.

9:27 a.m.—While attempting crossing of drainage ditch via rotting log—with advice of myself, M executes perfect two-and-a-half gainer from the tuck position off said log and into ditch. Being the only available judges, Dog and I score dive at a 7.5, no degree of difficulty. M emerges from ditch encrusted with mud, pouring water from gun barrels. Using camera I keep for such occasions, I record incident for posterity. M curses ditch, log, Self, and Nikon camera company.

10:04 a.m.—Spying a grouse perched in an apple tree, M, Self, and Dog stalk nearer in anticipation of shooting when grouse flushes. Grouse chooses to remain in tree, sensing we will not fire at perched bird. What grouse does not know is that he is safe in flying, because we are lousy shots.

Regardless, attempts at hurling sticks, stones, apples, and expletives fail to dislodge bird. M finally moves closer to shake low-hanging limb. Grouse chooses this instant to release three days' worth of solid excrement onto M's hat brim. M calls grouse names that I have not heard since working on the docks between college semesters. Grouse knows an insult when he hears it, and flaps away. Four shots ring out, and grouse continues unscathed to land in nearby apple tree. We do not follow: M is too angry, and I cannot see clearly due to tear-shrouded vision.

11:42 a.m.—As midday approaches, we drive into nearest town to get some lunch at a diner called "Mom's." Mom is in attendance and bars M's entry, citing color and odor of M's clothing from recent excursion into ditch. M points out that this odor would be a marked improvement over smells emanating from Mom's kitchen. Mom orders M out, but I stay to order two cheeseburgers to go. Arriving back at the shooting car, I toss M's burger to him from passenger's seat. Dog, leaning over from the back seat, picks off burger with ease of an NFL flanker, and burger promptly joins my woodcock in Dog's digestive tract. M uses words I've never heard before to describe Dog, her gastronomical gymnastics, and her preceding three generations.

12:08 p.m.—We drive to next cover dubbed the Old Homestead, so named as M located old basement two seasons ago. Unfortunately, M determined it was a basement from the horizontal position looking up. Dog points a woodcock at base of birch clump. I miss both barrels, but make dog look for nonexistent bird. M and Dog both claim I am liar. They are, of course, correct.

12:43 p.m.—By foot, we investigate Wild Boar cover, so named because five years ago Dog pointed a sow and six suckling pigs in a patch of blackberry vines, a feat I remind M of on each visit of the last five years. M claims woodcock are on hillside; I claim they are in swamp. Dog points woodcock in half-picked cornfield while we argue. M runs over and shoots bird, which Dog intends to eat to tamp down snack of previous woodcock and burger. Fight ensues. M wrestles dog amongst cornstalks, emerging victorious, even though I offer advice to Dog. I am laughing until my sides ache as M curses Dog, Me, and what is left of woodcock. We leave this cover.

1:04 p.m.—Arriving at the Pasture Cover, we ask permission to hunt from crusty old farmer. We are never denied such permission because sadistic farmer enjoys watching city hunters try to negotiate 40-acre pasture to gain access to a 5-acre patch of alders and aspen located in center of pasture. Pasture is indisputable domain of an Angus bull with the disposition of Adolph Eichmann, and the physical attributes of average-sized GMC tractor.

1:10 p.m.—Chase is joined, as Bull spots our intrusion. We break for the cover, and Bull makes for M, who is slowed by mud-encrusted clothing, vis-a-vis the ditch at 9:27 a.m. As I pound for safety of the patch of cover, it occurs to me that Bull especially hates M and would gladly swear off heifers and trundle up south face of Matterhorn for one decent shot at M. Obviously, Bull is perceptive creature, and my estimation of this animal grows. Under pressure, M has open field moves like O. J. Simpson, and we gain the safety of the cover one-half second ahead of $1\frac{1}{2}$ tons of black fury.

1:12 p.m.—Knowing the routine by rote, Bull ambles to the end of the cover to await our arrival. We hunt out the cover, and move no birds. Spotting Bull at the end of the cover, we caucus to play strategy about the time the skies open up with monsoonlike deluge. We decide that Bull will grow weary of waiting in the rain, and return from the field of combat for safety of barn. Glancing at barn, we notice that farmer has invited over neighbors who have set up lawn chairs under eaves of that building to witness drama, and crowd sentiments are running for the Bull.

2:43 p.m.—Unable to stand rain any longer, and seeing that Bull means to wait us out, we elect to make a run for it. M breaks left. I head right, aiming for safety of barnyard. Wild cheer goes up from the crowd. Cleansed of mud, M stretches out lead over Bull, who switches targets and comes for me.

2:45 p.m.—Bull is gaining as my temples throb from exertion and breathing becomes shallow and labored. Safety beyond electric fence beckons invitingly, and I am verbally encouraged by M, who has already gained safety. Bull is verbally encouraged by occupants of barn. Leaping over electric fence, I miscalculate my ability, wet footing, and fence's height, coming down astraddle it. My clothes are wet; juice is on. I curse Bull, farmer, fence, and Benjamin Franklin. Bull takes out frustrations on my hunting hat, dropped at midpoint of latest dash. Cheers from the barn.

2:50 p.m.—Thoroughly bushed, we head home, thankful for the chance to be outdoors on such a glorious day.

Steve Smith

Acknowledgments

Some of the materials in this book came from *A Hunter's Fireside Book* and *Mostly Tailfeathers*, both by Gene Hill. Other stories came from *The Whispering Wings of Autumn*, another Smith/Hill collaboration.

In addition, *Gun Dog* magazine and *The Drummer* were very helpful in granting permission to use pieces that have appeared there.

Finally, a thanks to our families who put up with us and prodded us when we had this book to write and would rather have been out grouse hunting.

To all of these folks, thanks.